Living Adult Education

Innovations in Education

Series Editor: Colin Fletcher (Senior Lecturer in the School of Policy Studies, Cranfield Institute of Technology).

There have been periods of major innovation in public education. What do the achievements amount to and what are the prospects for progress now? There are issues in each slice of the education sector. How have the issues come about?

Each author analyses their own sphere, argues from experience and communicates clearly. Here are books that speak both with and for the teaching profession; books that can be shared with all those involved in the future of education.

Three quotations have helped to shape the series:

The whole process – false starts, frustrations, adaptions, the successive recasting of intentions, the detours and conflicts – needs to be comprehended. Only then can we understand what has been achieved and learn from experience.

Marris and Rein

In this time of considerable educational change and challenge the need for teachers to write has never been greater.

Hargreaves

A wise innovator should prepare packages of programmes and procedures which . . . could be put into effect quickly in periods of recovery and reorganisation following a disaster.

Hirsh

Current titles in the series

Pat Ainley: *From School to YTS*
Garth Allen, John Bastiani, Ian Martin, Kelvyn Richards: *Community Education*
Bernard Barker: *Rescuing the Comprehensive Experience*
Julia Gilkes: *Developing Nursery Education*
Tony Jeffs and Mark Smith: *Using Informal Education*
Knud Jenson and Stephen Walker: *Towards Democratic Schooling*
Gerri Kirkwood and Colin Kirkwood: *Living Adult Education*
Herbert Kohl: *36 Children*
Julia Stanley: *Marks on the Memory*
Jan Stewart: *The Making of the Primary School*
David Terry: *The Tertiary College*
Paul Widlake: *Reducing Educational Disadvantage*

Living Adult Education

Freire in Scotland

Gerri Kirkwood
Colin Kirkwood

Open University Press
Published in association with the
Scottish Institute of Adult and Continuing Education

Open University Press
Celtic Court
22 Ballmoor
Buckingham MK18 1XW

and
1900 Frost Road, Suite 101
Bristol, PA 19007, USA

Published in association with the Scottish Institute of Adult and
Continuing Education.

First Published 1989   Reprinted 1990

Copyright © Scottish Institute of Adult and Continuing Education 1989

British Library Cataloguing in Publication Data

Kirkwood, Gerri
  Living adult education: Freire in Scotland. –
  (Innovations in education)
  1. Scottish. Adult education
  I. Title   II. Kirkwood, Colin
  III. Series
  374'.941

  ISBN 0-335-09556-9
  ISBN 0-335-09555-0 pbk

Library of Congress Cataloging in Publication Data

Kirkwood, Gerri.
    Living adult education: Freire in Scotland/Gerri Kirkwood,
  Colin Kirkwood.
      p.   cm. – (Innovations in education)
    Bibliography: p.
    Includes index.
    ISBN 0-335-09556-9.   ISBN 0-335-09555-0 (pbk.)
    1. Adult education – Scotland – Edinburgh – Case studies.
  2. Freire, Paulo, 1921–   . 3. Adult education – Philosophy.
  I. Kirkwood, Colin.   II. Title.   III. Series
  LC5256.S352E355   1989
  374'.9413'4 – dc19   88-26837   CIP

Typeset by Rowland Phototypesetting Limited
Bury St Edmunds, Suffolk
Printed in Great Britain by St Edmundsbury Press Limited
Bury St Edmunds, Suffolk

Contents

List of illustrations   vi
Acknowledgements   vii
Preface   ix
Introduction   xi

1   The story of ALP   1
2   Ideas and contexts   26
3   Investigations and learning programmes: case studies   47
4   Action outcomes and workshops: case studies   101
5   The influence of ALP   119
6   Reflections   133

Glossary   139
Select bibliography   146
Digest of statistics   147
Index   152

List of illustrations

1. Map of Gorgie Dalry   3
2. Orwell Terrace scene   5
3. The ALP process – a summary   7
4. The ALP tree – a summary of the story of ALP   16
5. An ALP learning group   49
6. Street scene with living room inset   53
7. A traditional and a modern classroom   55
8. An electronic component assembler   57
9. Mothers outside the school gate   58
10. Family in the street   59
11. After work – in the pub   60
12. View from the ALP shop with adverts   61
13. Scottish football fans at Wembley, 1977   63
14. Unemployment – at home   71
15. Women and Well-being leaflet   74
16. Women in conversation in the street   76
17. At the baby clinic – waiting   77
18. At the baby clinic – consultation with a doctor   78
19. Children learning to sew   84
20. Boys jumping off the weir at Cramond   85
21. Children playing in the street   87
22. Boys playing on bikes in the Terraces   103
23. Play in the Terraces campaign – open-air display   104
24. The Writers Workshop – a demonstration session   113

Acknowledgements

This book has been written in a Freirean spirit and is the product of complex layers of team work. We cannot therefore simply give a routine 'list of acknowledgements', but wish to pay tribute to all participants in the process in a more personal way.

First there are the *creators* of the book. At the heart of the enterprise lies the collaboration of the two authors, Gerri and Colin Kirkwood, both adult educators and also marital partners. Gerri researched the book and originated the text, except for Chapter 2 and the glossary of terms, which were Colin's work. At the editorial stage, Colin reworked the drafts, but in consultation with Gerri, so it was, as she says, 'a married couple job'.

Gerri has been a member of the Adult Learning Project (ALP) team from the beginning and worked very closely with Stan Reeves and Mike Rosendale in her research and preparation of drafts, discussing all the issues with them. And Gerri, Colin, Stan and Mike were also members of the Project Committee, which was convened by the Scottish Institute of Adult and Continuing Education (SIACE). The other members were: Gerry Cairns, Lothian Region; Brian Semple, Scottish Education Department; and Elisabeth Gerver and Lalage Bown, SIACE. The committee acted as a sounding board for the authors' ideas and discussed issues, texts and format with them. All found it an absorbing and stimulating experience.

As well as the visible teams (the author partners; the ALP workers; the Project Committee) there was a less determinate team, made up of all participants in ALP over the years, whose presence, views and achievements decided the existence and shape of the book.

Secondly, there are the *providers of resources* – the Scottish Education Department, who imaginatively gave a grant to SIACE to fund this book's preparation, and Lothian Regional Council, who allowed Gerri Kirkwood to use her time in the necessary research and writing. Honour is very much due to Lothian Regional Council for having continued to support ALP through the years.

Thirdly, there are the many *people who have contributed specialist skills* to ALP and to the book itself. These have included interviewers of ALP participants and the various ALP assessors, consultants and resource persons. In particular, the various teams valued and appreciated the contributions of: Joan Bree, who did all the typing; Mary McCann and Jo Hignett who illustrated the leaflets; Julie Macdonald and Davy Hunter who prepared the map of Gorgie Dalry; Sandra McSheaffrey who undertook the initial research in the ALP chronofile; the ALP Photo Workshop who did the photographic codifications and Janet McLaughlin who did the sketched codifications. The *Scotsman* newspaper permitted the use of the photograph of the 1977 Wembley football match.

Thanks to the help and goodwill of all these people and to the clear understanding of the Kirkwoods, it is our faith that this book conveys the authentic voice of ALP.

Lalage Bown

Preface

The Gorgie Dalry Adult Learning Project in Edinburgh, known affectionately as ALP, is a sustained experiment in applying the principles of the Brazilian adult educationist, Paulo Freire, in a Western European post-industrial urban environment. After almost ten years, it has become an accepted and highly respected feature of the adult education landscape in Scotland, operating throughout under the auspices of the local authority and constantly visited by enquirers and students.

ALP's prime importance is to the community of Gorgie Dalry and the many members of that community who have participated in its work and have gained heightened awareness in learning programmes there. But its unique character and history make it of serious interest to adult educators all over Britain and elsewhere as well. This book is partly a celebration of its achievements and partly a bid to spread knowledge of its work more widely.

One reason for ALP's significance is that it is an experiment in cultural borrowing, an acknowledgement that UK adult educators need to escape from insularity and recognize the possible value of theories and methods engendered in 'the South' – to use the Brandt Commission's shorthand for developing countries. We and they are now facing similar challenges – large-scale unemployment and under-employment, social fragmentation, sharp inequalities between rich and poor, urban stress and decay – and if we perceive adult education as a tool for change, adult educators in North and South can only gain if they exchange ideas and try them out in each other's environments.

Freire is fairly well known in Britain, in the sense that some of his more general ideas about, for instance, the combination of reflection and action (praxis) are part of the rhetoric of adult educationists; but full-scale, consistent efforts to apply his theory as a whole are very rare. Hence the second reason for the importance of ALP. The Freirean process has been worked through over a sufficient length of time for the practitioners involved to say that it works and it has value and others in Britain should be challenged to try it.

Thirdly, in saying that it works, the ALP team are affirming a constructive and vigorous alternative to some of the current orthodoxies being pushed in adult education by some government agencies – the kind of orthodoxies which were described recently by a disillusioned further education lecturer in England: 'in tomorrow's world of testing, training and technology . . . all students can sit passively and contentedly as "docile listeners in the transfer of information", free from the discomfort of participating'. Cheryl Law – Farewell to Freire, *Adult Education*, 60/4, March 1988, Leicester, National Institute of Adult and Continuing Education (NIACE). There can be discomfort in participating, but the long-term results in terms of human and social transformation are surely a vindication.

Because this book explains so sensitively the theory and rationale of Freirean education, it will provide a first-rate grounding for those who want it; and because it describes so carefully the Freirean process at work in a Western setting, it should hearten and inspire all those who fear the iron hold of mechanistic and passive approaches to learning. It is thorough, serious and exciting and tells the story of a thorough, serious and exciting experiment.

Lalage Bown
Convenor, ALP Book Project Committee,
Scottish Institute of Adult and Continuing Education

Introduction

The writings of the Brazilian adult educator, Paulo Freire, have been available in English as a source of inspiration and encouragement to students, teachers and trainers since the early 1970s. In spite of the cultural gap between Brazil and Britain, and the difficulty of his language, we knew that Freire was speaking to us.

Interest in his work has grown steadily. Today there are few writers on adult education who do not acknowledge his influence. Freire has been no instantly disposable prophet.

Yet all along there has been a problem. Although, from time to time, word was out that such and such a project was struggling to apply his ideas, after the initial flurry of excitement, little further information would emerge. It was as if the gap was too wide to bridge. It was as if Freire belonged to another world. He faced south, towards Africa and Latin America, and although he visited North America and many European countries, and for ten years was based at the World Council of Churches in Geneva, doubts were expressed as to the relevance of his interesting ideas about oppression, liberation, and the culture of silence in the high-tech democracies of the north.

The opposite view was also held, that Freire was saying nothing that was not embodied in the work of the best exponents of the liberal tradition in British adult education.

For whatever reasons, it seemed that his vision and our reality were doomed to remain apart.

In the Lothian Region of Scotland, as elsewhere, there was an existing interest in Freire's ideas among community education workers, which was further encouraged by a series of courses offered by the Workers' Educational Association. It was this interest which led to the successful efforts of Fraser Patrick (Community Education Officer) and Douglas Shannon (Senior Community Education Worker) to obtain funding for a project which would put his ideas into practice.

This book tells the story of how, in 1979, the Adult Learning Project (ALP) came to be created, as a systematic attempt to implement Freire's approach in Scotland. It sets out to explain his ideas as simply as possible, and to show how they have been adapted and applied by the ALP workers and participants in learning programmes in the Gorgie Dalry area of Edinburgh.

It is written by practitioners for practitioners, trainers, managers and policy makers, and tries to answer the questions which have been directed at the ALP workers over the years. The authors have attempted to communicate the experience of taking part in Freire-type learning groups, the process that has been developed, the issues that have arisen, and the lessons that have been learned. They have tried to represent the contributions of everyone: ALP workers, participants, and resource people. It has been a difficult but rewarding job.

Chapter 1 tells the story of the ALP project, its origins, the locality in which it is set, the staff employed, and the process of learning and action generated from Freire's ideas.

Chapter 2 deals with ideas, the British context, the context of education and specifically of community education, and concludes with an account of Paulo Freire's life, his ideas, and the methods he developed in Brazil and Chile.

Chapter 3 consists of case studies of three major ALP investigations; *Living in Gorgie Dalry*, *Health and Well-being*, and *Parents and Authority*, and the learning programmes emerging from them.

Chapter 4 presents case studies of three action outcomes arising from the learning programmes described in Chapter 3: *Play in the Terraces*, the *Skills Exchange*, and the *Parents Centre*, followed by two ALP groups whose activities have been central to the vitality of the project, the *Photo Workshop* and the *Writers Workshop*.

Chapter 5 discusses the influence of ALP on participants, on the staff, and on other professionals, drawing on interviews and on the project's records of its training work.

Chapter 6 offers some reflections on what has made ALP thrive, and explores key themes recurring throughout the life of the project which have wider implications for the spread of the influence of Freire and of ALP.

Since ALP is an ideas-intensive project, and since many of these ideas are difficult – or at any rate, unfamiliar – a glossary has been included with definitions of terms used by Freire or by ALP. The first time each word is used in the text, it is in italics, encouraging the reader to refer to the glossary for clarification if necessary.

The book concludes with a select bibliography and a statistical summary of participation in ALP over the period from 1979–87. Illustrations are included throughout.

ALP is a part of the Community Education Service of Lothian Regional Council. A word of explanation about the meaning of community education in Scotland may be helpful. The Community Education Service was established in the years after 1975, following the publication of Alexander Report which recommended the integration of adult education and youth and community work into a single service. It is promoted at national level by the Scottish Community Education Council. The specific interests of adult education in community, further, and higher education, and in the voluntary sector, are promoted by the Scottish Institute of Adult and Continuing Education.

ALP was set up in the first place as an Urban Aid project. Essentially this means that it was financed jointly by central government (the Scottish Education Department) and local government (Lothian Regional Council) on a 75/25 per cent basis. After an initial three-year period of funding, a two-year extension was given. At the end of five years, Urban Aid projects sponsored by local government either close down, or else the local government body involved assumes full financial responsibility, integrating the project into its own mainstream provision. The campaign by ALP participants to secure the future of the project in Gorgie Dalry received widespread support from adult education bodies throughout Britain, and was successful.

ALP continues to thrive, and can be contacted at 184 Dalry Road, Edinburgh, telephone number 031 337 5442.

This book is a project of the Scottish Institute of Adult and Continuing Education, supported by Lothian Regional Council, and funded by the Scottish Education Department. The views expressed, however, are those of the authors, and not of the sponsoring organizations.

CHAPTER 1

The story of ALP

Origins and aims

The Adult Learning Project in Gorgie Dalry was started in 1977 by a small group of women supported by a neighbourhood community worker and a community education worker. A street-based survey was carried out, asking people what classes they would like. The demand was for classes such as English 'O' grade and yoga. They were to be free, put on at times and places convenient to residents, and managed by local people. Tutors were to be responsive in their approach, prepared to negotiate the content of programmes with students. Initially, tutors were paid, but the idea was that some students would themselves become volunteer tutors.

The community education worker hoped that, as an atmosphere of learning developed in the area, people would begin to explore personal, local and national issues in a more systematic way.

This early ALP, then, was based on ideas of self-reliance, popular demand, local access and local control. It was quickly successful, with nearly 200 people taking part in the first year. Already demand was outstripping resources in the form of the time the women and the community education worker were able to give to the project, and the money available to pay part-time tutors.

Lothian Region's Community Education Department, with the agreement of the women, made an application for urban aid funding to the Scottish Office. They asked for three community education workers, a secretary/receptionist, a shop on the main road, and a budget for books, publicity, tutors' fees, and equipment. The stated aims were to provide cheap learning opportunities locally, in response to requests; to create a network of local tutors; to develop issue-based education; and to publicize the project effectively.

During the following year, while the urban aid application was being processed, changes took place as a result of which these aims were modified. Community education staff were deepening their interest in the work of Paulo Freire, and joined an in-service training course on his ideas and methods organized by the Workers' Educational Association (WEA). The influence of Freire led to a shift away from the idea of classes provided in response to popular demand, towards programmes aimed at exploring themes and concerns identified by residents. In practice, this meant moving away from vocational and leisure-and-recreation classes towards issue-based education. Classes would still be provided in the area, but by other community education workers, outside the framework of ALP.

The proposed role of the full-time workers was also changed in emphasis, from responding to demand, organizing classes and supporting volunteer tutors, to playing a key part in every stage of what later came to be called the ALP process: *investigation*, building *learning programmes*, and supporting *action outcomes*.*

Gorgie Dalry: The place and the people

Gorgie Dalry is a densely populated inner area of Edinburgh, sandwiched between the west end of the city centre and the suburbs. Built between 1880 and 1900 for the families of workers employed on the railways and in local factories, it was for years solidly working class. People lived close to where they worked. The area was the centre of their social life. Hearts Football Club had its home here – and still does.

In the 1960s this picture was disturbed when many families moved out to Wester Hailes and other peripheral council housing schemes. Local works closed down – the rubber mill, the biscuit factory, a glue works, laundries, engineering works, the railway sheds. Breweries like Scottish and Newcastle became automated and needed fewer workers. Other employers like Ferrantis required a highly skilled workforce and recruited from all over Lothian, not just locally.

---

* The first mention of terms used by Freire or ALP are in italics in the text and defined in the Glossary (see pp 139–45).

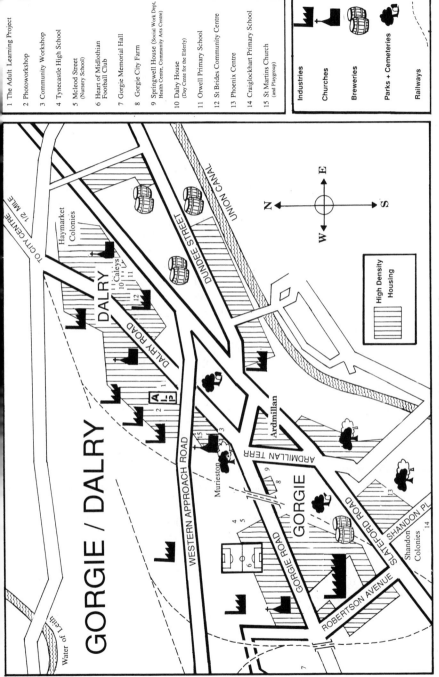

1. Map of Gorgie Dalry

1   The Adult Learning Project
2   Photoworkshop
3   Community Workshop
4   Tynecastle High School
5   Mcleod Street
    (Nursery School)
6   Heart of Midlothian
    Football Club
7   Gorgie Memorial Hall
8   Gorgie City Farm
9   Springwell House (Social Work Dept,
    Health Centre, Community Arts Centre)
10 Dalry House
    (Day Cente for the Elderly)
11 Orwell Primary School
12 St Brides Community Centre
13 Phoenix Centre
14 Craiglockhart Primary School
15 St Martins Church
    (and Playgroup)

Industries

Churches

Breweries

Parks + Cemeteries

Railways

Today, Gorgie Dalry is not one community but several. The old population of skilled and unskilled working class people remains, reduced in numbers. But new people have been moving in, attracted by the relative cheapness of the housing and its nearness to the city centre. Many residents now work elsewhere, and many of those who work locally live elsewhere. The majority of existing working class residents are middle aged to elderly, while most of the incomers are younger, often with more education and white collar jobs. Some are single, some couples without children, some have one young child. The percentage of households with children is small. In the last few years there has been an influx of young unemployed people, sharing rented accommodation.

Despite these population changes, the physical character of the place and its reputation for friendliness remains intact. First impressions are of a crowded area of tenements, small shops, factories and breweries, churches, schools and other public buildings, on either side of a busy main road. The narrow side streets are lined with parked cars, many belonging to people working in the area or in the nearby city centre rather than to residents. The smell from the breweries and the noise of the traffic are constant factors. There is an impression of lack of greenery, in spite of the Victorian graveyard on the main road (hidden behind a high wall), the small park in the Muriestons, and the Gorgie City Farm.

The whole place has a feeling of being on the move. Rehabilitation of the housing stock by Gorgie Dalry Housing Association and Edinburgh District Council, begun in the late 1970s, is well advanced. Tenants, owner occupiers and private landlords are benefiting, despite the stress and upheaval of decanting or living on a building site. Many environmental problems remain, like the smallness of the flats and the lack of play space for children, but – despite grumblings – these seem to be accepted, along with the benefits, as part of the cost of living so close to the city centre.

Some important distinctions are not obvious to outsiders. Gorgie and Dalry are two distinct areas, separated by the traffic junction at Ardmillan Terrace. Defining other boundaries is not so easy. Shandon, an area of terraced houses with small gardens just up the hill, can be considered part of Gorgie or of Merchiston, depending on where you send your children to school, do your shopping, and feel you belong.

2. Orwell Terrace scene

The ALP workers

Gerri Kirkwood, Stan Reeves and Fiona O'Kane started as ALP workers in September 1979. Joan Bree, the ALP secretary and receptionist, arrived six months later. All are still in post, except for Fiona, who left in 1984.

Their backgrounds are very different. Gerri is married with two teenage children. She has a degree in modern languages, and post-graduate training in adult education and community development, and human relations and counselling. She has previous experience as a teacher, community worker, reporter to children's panels, and tutor on return to learning courses. Stan is married with two school-age children. He trained as a photographer and then as a youth and community worker. He has previously been an adventure playground organizer and a community development worker. He also plays the melodeon in a ceilidh band. Fiona is married and has a degree in English language and literature, with postgraduate training in community education. She has previously worked as a literacy tutor/organizer, and is now in mainstream community education. All three had prior interest in the work of Paulo Freire. Joan Bree is single. She trained as a secretary and has previously worked in a bank and as a mother's help in Canada.

The ALP process

What follows is an outline of the ALP process of building programmes of learning and action as it has been refined during the life of the project. Its evolution is examined in detail in the case studies presented later. This represents ALP workers' understanding of Paulo Freire's approach to education as they have adapted it in Gorgie Dalry in the 1980s.

The stages in the process are:

secondary source investigation
primary source investigation
finding *co-investigators*
co-investigation
building *codifications*
decoding
building the curriculum
learning programmes
action outcomes

Secondary source investigation

The workers begin by doing research on the life of the area using secondary sources, that is material written about it available from local and central government departments, libraries, universities, and so on. They meet regularly to share their findings and begin to build up a composite picture, which may include such dimensions as the built environment, work, schooling, planning, census information, health profile, employment and unemployment, and so on.

Primary source investigation

The workers get to know the area at first hand by walking about and observing the physical environment and the way people relate to each other in public. They make contact with key professionals,

who	stage	how
ALP workers and coinvestigators	[10] New investigation	repeat process
participants in learning programmes and other residents	[9] Action outcomes	community action around problem; create new organisation; personal outcomes
open invitation to residents	[8] Learning programmes	recruit participants, say your own word, presentation by expert, dialogue
the ALP workers, coinvestigators, and experts/resource persons	[7] Building the curriculum	construct thematic programme, brief experts/resource persons
as previous, plus open invitation to residents	[6] Decoding	discuss codifications in groups, using questions, identify themes and contradictions
as previous	[5] Building codifications	select and clarify situations, brief artists/photographers, choose sequence
the ALP workers, with residents volunteering to be coinvestigators	[4] Coinvestigation	interview neighbours, observe moments of life, discuss findings
the ALP workers	[3] Finding coinvestigators	knock doors, hold public meetings, recruit from ALP membership
as previous	[2] Primary source investigation	walk the area, contact professionals, community organisations, etc
at first, the ALP workers, later residents/coinvestigators	[1] Secondary source investigation	visit libraries, local and central government departments, universities, etc

who ○ stage ○ how

3. ALP process – a summary

clergy, the local politicians, and residents involved in community organizations. They visit workplaces and make contact with managers and with trade unionists.

The questions asked in this stage are: how do people see the area, its boundaries, its physical and social characteristics, its history? What are their feelings about the area and their hopes for its future? What is their personal experience and knowledge of its problems? The aim is to build up a picture of the people, the area, its background and its difficulties as experienced by those who live and work there, to set beside the factual information gathered from secondary sources.

Finding co-investigators

The next task is to invite a cross-section of residents to join the workers in the investigation process. At the beginning of ALP this was done by knocking on people's doors, explaining the purpose of the project and inviting them to attend a public meeting. Once the project got into its stride, co-investigators were recruited from those who had participated in earlier ALP programmes.

Co-investigation

The co-investigators meet regularly with the ALP workers, one of whom leads the group with the other as *observer/recorder*. Co-investigators are invited to say how they experience life in the area. The aim is not to come to conclusions but to formulate questions which the co-investigators in their turn will ask other people.

In general ALP workers and local volunteers share all the tasks of this stage. Co-investigators interview their own contacts in the area: relatives, neighbours, shopkeepers, and so on. These interviews take the form of conversations: the co-investigator takes notes or may use a taperecorder, asking a series of broad open questions and paying particular attention to matters of special concern to the individual being interviewed.

Another dimension of co-investigation is the observation of moments of life. This involves visits to public places in the locality where people come together. Participants are encouraged to make these visits in pairs, to overcome diffidence. Where visits are made to settings attended by members only, some advance preparation may be necessary. The purpose is to observe the nature of the activities, how they are organized, the communications between participants, including the words, phrases and gestures used, and the emotional content of the encounters. Co-investigators are given guidance on how to observe but not what to find. Co-investigators continue to meet as a group to share their findings with one another. One ALP worker listens for common concerns, linking interviews and observations together. The meetings are taperecorded so that no important material is lost. The aim now is to begin to identify key *themes* which will be codified at the next stage.

The worker leading the group encourages people to report back from their interviews and observations. The data often comes back in the form of stories interviewees have told to illustrate a point. The leader invites responses from other co-investigators to the material presented, sometimes summarizing and *re-presenting* what has been said to let people hear the evidence more clearly and begin to reflect on it. Towards the end of the session, the observer, who has been listening and taking notes, feeds back observations of the group process and the themes beginning to emerge. Co-investigators in their turn comment on these observations. Finally, the programme of interviews and observations to be carried out before the next meeting is agreed.

After the meeting the ALP workers, drawing on the notes and taperecordings, tentatively identify significant statements that have been made and themes that are emerging. This is typed up, given to co-investigators at the next meeting, and checked out with them. By the end of this stage, a number of themes have been named as they exist in the *significant situations* of people's experience.

Building codifications

The task now is to find a way of illustrating these themes in their social settings. The co-investigators are asked to describe the situations in which a theme first emerged. What was the setting? What was happening at the time? Who were the actors in the situation? How were they relating to one another? Out of this brainstorm, a series of briefs for codifications is prepared.

ALP has experimented with different media for codifying themes. At first, a local artist was asked to prepare drawings, schematic representations of a theme presented in several situations simultaneously. Later she was asked to make a more realistic representation of a situation, showing elements of the physical environment and the relationships of people to each other and to the situation itself. The advantage of a drawing is that it is a composition by the artist, who can include all the elements necessary for understanding the situation in one image. It was soon found, however, that drawings have their problems. People see them as art. They are distracted by the style and quality of the drawing, and whether or not it is an accurate representation. They also expect the artist to interpret reality for them.

Photography has proved to be a more suitable medium for ALP's purposes, though also not without problems. Most people take photographs for granted as mirroring reality. They know that the photographer has selected both image and viewpoint, but as a medium it does not intrude. People tend to read photographs the same way as they read reality. The main problem is that the photographer is limited by what the camera can include at any one moment and this may exclude some of the elements necessary for understanding the totality of a situation. The problem can be overcome by using several photographs. Good photographic codifications are really powerful tools enabling *dialogue* to take place.

A codification should not be too enigmatic, so that those respond-ing to it in a group will be able to find themselves in it and interpret it in the light of their own experience; nor too explicit, otherwise the group is deprived of the task of interpretation.

For the purposes of codification, the photographer, like the artist, is given a brief describing the situation, the elements to be contained in the image and the relationships of the elements to each other and to the whole. The photographer is asked to capture the significant moment, or *peak of action*, in the situation.

At later stages in the development of ALP, other media have been used for making codifications, including taperecorded interviews, articles from books and newspapers, videotapes, TV programmes and adverts, slides, poems and various combinations of these.

The next task is to make a selection of codifications and arrange them in a sequence which will allow participants involved in decod-ing to make connections between the themes and *contradictions* contained in each codification and in the sequence as a whole.

Decoding

Other residents are now invited to join in discussions around the codifications. The co-investigators invite people they have inter-viewed. Carefully designed publicity reaches out to those with first-hand experience of the situations to be explored, to members of community organizations, passers by, and anyone else who may be interested.

Several decoding groups of 10 or 12 are formed, meeting at different times of the day to allow a wide cross-section of residents to become involved. An ALP worker leads each group, with the help of another worker or a co-investigator whose role is to observe and record.

At the start of the first session the co-ordinator explains the purpose of decoding and the methods to be used. It is an opportunity to take a closer look at some familiar situations and say what you think. The success of the discussion depends on participants being prepared to share their experience of the situation with others in the group. The outcome of all these discussions will be the creation of learning and action programmes to tackle some of the issues raised.

The first codification is displayed on an easel. Participants sit round it in a semicircle. The co-ordinator asks a series of open questions designed to take people gradually into an analysis of the situation. A sequence of questions has been prepared in advance, but others are added as the dialogue in the group begins to take shape.

The first level of questions is simply descriptive. The group is invited to look at the picture and describe everything they see in it. They are encouraged to break the image down into its elements.

The next level of questions invites participants to identify with people in the situation. They are encouraged to read their expressions, postures and gestures, and suggest what their relationships to each other and to the situation might be. Since the situation is a familiar one, members are able to fill the picture out from their own experience.

The following levels are more challenging. Members are invited to relate the situation to their own lives, to place themselves in it. Then they are asked why the situation is as they have described it. This question encourages them to look beyond the particular and the personal to wider social, political, cultural and historical factors.

Themes and contradictions emerge throughout the session. Sometimes the co-ordinator intervenes to re-present what is beginning to emerge, choosing her moments carefully, so as not to interrupt the flow of discussion. She may draw together common threads in what people are saying, or move things on by posing further questions.

The process of communication in the group moves gradually

from the responses of individuals, often directed at the co-ordinator, to dialogue in which members respond to each other's comments and begin to formulate their own questions.

One of the problems is keeping the group together, getting them to build on each other's contributions co-operatively. The codification helps by acting as a focus. The co-ordinator's skill in re-presenting what she hears and addressing questions to the whole group is also important. But the difficulty of keeping a balance between individual and group remains. The tension is particularly acute in this method, because the co-ordinator wants to encourage individuals to express themselves and value their experience, and at the same time to value the experience of others by listening and responding to their contributions.

At the end of each decoding session, the observer is invited to contribute. From his notes he outlines the key points of the discussion, quoting from what individuals have said. Key words and phrases may be written on the flip chart. He then offers to the group any themes or contradictions he has spotted which have been missed in the heat of discussion. The group responds, confirming or challenging the observer's comments and adding their own points.

Finally, the co-ordinator checks out if it is possible to get agreement in the group about what has been the most important theme to emerge in the discussion.

A written record is made of each session and if possible posted out to members before the next meeting. It includes a distillation of the discussion, the themes and contradictions emerging, and the observer's comments on how the session went. At the end of the sequence of decoding discussions, the recordings are gathered together and used as the basis for a final workshop, where the task is to identify the most generative themes and to brief the ALP workers about the content of the curriculum.

Building the curriculum

The brief is the outcome of all the work done in co-investigation and decoding. People's concerns have been identified and their feelings about them explored. They have looked beneath the surface of taken-for-granted situations and begun to see them afresh, and in a wider context. They have identified themes requiring further *action reflection*.

The task now is to construct a thematic programme which will try to address different levels of reality simultaneously: personal, local, national, global. It will try to take account of the inner world of feelings and the outer world of facts, the influence of the past, the impact of the present and the potential for the future.

Such a programme can cut across the boundaries of subject disciplines. Appropriate experts are approached – for example, a psychologist, a historian, a political economist. They are given a detailed brief covering the exploration carried out so far and the questions which have arisen. They are asked how they would address these themes from the point of view of their own discipline. And the ALP process and their potential role in it is explained. The aim is to create a programme which will be a seamless garment. At early stages in the life of ALP the workers sometimes found it hard to give a clear enough brief, and some of the experts were unused to building interdisciplinary programmes and working dialogically. ALP is still struggling creatively with these challenges.

Learning programmes

Programmes usually run to 8 or 10 weekly sessions each lasting 1½ to 2 hours. The importance of attending each meeting in the sequence is stressed, and participants are asked to make this commitment. For daytime sessions in which parents with small children are involved, a creche is provided.

At each meeting group members have the first word. The ALP worker triggers the process by asking a key question arising out of decoding, which underlies the invitation to this particular expert. The expert then makes her presentation, based on the brief agreed beforehand with the worker, and adjusted to take into account what group members have just been saying.

Finally there is a dialogue, in which all take part in what Freire calls a mutual search for truth. The task here is to integrate the expert's knowledge and experience with the group's previous knowledge and experience. The ALP worker's role is to facilitate the dialogue. Problems can arise here from the compulsion of some experts to talk too much, and the tendency of some group members to become passive in the presence of experts. Much depends on the way the session has been set up, the facilitating role of the worker, and the expert's ability to respond quickly and sensitively.

Action outcomes

Participants know from the outset that some kind of action is a hoped-for outcome from the learning programmes. The action itself can be of different kinds. It may involve community action by the group in co-operation with other local people to tackle a specific problem, the creation of a new community organization in the area, or action by individuals in their own lives. Changes in attitudes occurring during the learning programmes may result in people deciding to stay where they are in a positive sense.

There may be gains in self-knowledge, self acceptance, personal effectiveness and social functioning. There is no way of predicting what the outcomes of learning programmes will be. Workers cannot – and should not – always know the personal outcomes for individuals.

What we can say is that any action by the group in which the ALP worker is involved will always be characterized by prior investigation of the feasibility of the project, and continuing reflection on the process of action as it evolves.

The evolving process

Over the years the ALP process has become more flexible:

- the different stages can be of longer or shorter duration
- action can follow reflection or occur alongside it
- the process is often shortened and speeded up
- what is being investigated is clearly defined and can be limited in scope
- co-investigators are trained in the skills of interviewing and formulating questions
- each stage of the process has become more distinct – and more clearly linked to the following stage
- experts are integrated more fully into the learning process, often acting as resource persons or consultants to the group rather than as guest speakers
- group members themselves are asked to take on more responsibility for their own learning: building codifications, identifying key themes, recording the main points of the discussion, contributing ideas for the content of learning programmes, and leading their own action projects.

The story of ALP

The work of the ALP project over eight years divides into three phases, which reflect the struggle to adapt Freire's ideas in a western context, and also the funding arrangements. These phases can be named *the cauldron, the bridge,* and *maturity.* Many of the programmes mentioned below are dealt with later as case studies.

Phase one: the cauldron (1979–82)

The cauldron covers the first three years of urban aid funding, and is a period of experimentation and direction-finding. It is so-called because of the heat, the conflict of ideas and pressures, the explosiveness, and the uncertain alchemy of the brew!

Once the ALP workers were in post, the Community Education Officer (CEO) and the Senior Community Education Worker organized a three-week training course for them, which centred on close reading of *Pedagogy of the Oppressed* (Freire 1972). Through discussion of this text the workers began to struggle towards a common understanding of Freire's ideas and his methods, grappling with the words he uses in order to forge their own principles and a language for the project. In this process they started to become a team.

At first they had no permanent base and found themselves camping out in other community education premises, from which they carried out the processes of secondary and primary source investigation. Local reaction to their advent was mixed. The four women volunteers in the original project were unsure of their roles now that professional workers had arrived. Others resented the tag of deprived area which had provided the funding. There was some reluctance to invest in a short term project, puzzlement as to its educational objectives, and distrust of its experimental nature. People were keen to impress on the ALP workers how much was already being done by local organizations.

From the start it was decided that ALP should make special efforts to recruit residents who were not already involved in community organizations. For this reason and to ensure that the project became well rooted, the workers carried out a systematic programme of door knocking in the streets around the future ALP base, which had now been earmarked, to explain the aims of the project and recruit co-investigators. In this way, the first major investigation, called Living in Gorgie Dalry, got under way. It was a very broad

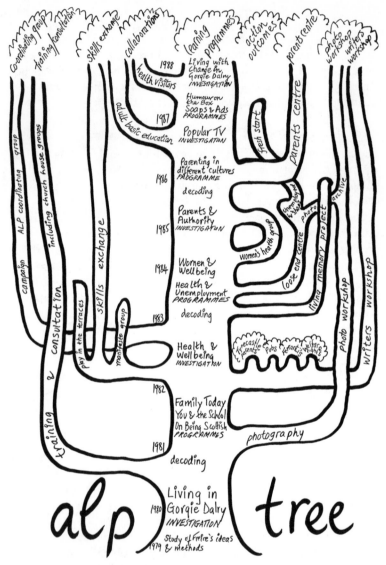

4. The ALP tree – a summary of the story of ALP

investigation lasting six months and it laid the basis for much of the work undertaken later in the project. It revealed Gorgie Dalry as a more fragmented community than at first appeared, anxiety among residents about some of the changes which were going on, and feelings of isolation and alienation.

It led on to the first experiments with various media for making codifications, the final choice of photography, and to the first decoding discussions which identified such themes as barriers to communication between parents and teachers, polarization between different social groups, and difficulties in dealing with authority figures and officialdom. The underlying theme was defined as the powerlessness of individuals to effect change in society.

Learning programmes created out of this process were The Family Today, You and the School, and On Being Scottish.

The action outcomes picked up on concrete problems which had emerged. Issues of housing density and lack of playspace for children led to the Play in the Terraces campaign. Redundancy, unemployment and their effects on family relationships led to the setting up of the Skills Exchange as a new organization. The first cuts in local government services led to the Manifesto Group whose members wrote a popular manifesto of principles and policies for education, housing, employment and the environment.

This two year process of investigation, decoding, learning programmes and action outcomes was punctuated by various events. First there was a move from one temporary base to another, and then, in September 1980, came the move into the ALP Shop where the project has been based ever since. It is a corner shop on the main Dalry Road, consisting of one large room, 32 feet by 16 feet, with enormous plate glass windows at the front and along one side. The space is divided by bookshelves and chairs into an area of learning groups, a playcorner for children, a materials production zone, a kitchen unit, a reception area, and desks for the workers.

A shop was chosen because ease of access to adult education opportunities was a key feature of the thinking behind the project. It has served that objective well. But right from the start its multi-purpose nature has been problematic as well as advantageous. Perhaps this is inevitable with a space which is simultaneously functioning as a drop-in centre, a quiet room for a learning group, a place for workers to plan programmes or produce materials, an office, and a creche!

About 18 months into the first phase, ALP's managers were

feeling a sense of urgency about the length of time it was taking to complete all the stages of the ALP process. They held a seminar attended by education officers, adult and community educators and politicians from throughout Scotland, who had been invited to inspect progress. An HMI expressed concern at what he saw as ALP's reliance on a single strategy. These pressures led to an intervention by the CEO who argued that there was too much pressure to bring people into the shop to take part in structured programmes. He wanted the methods which were being developed applied in outreach settings as well.

While the action outcomes arising from the first learning programmes proceeded, experimental work using interviews and codifications began with people in pubs, parents of children at Tynecastle High School, and workers in Ferrantis. A group of unemployed people were trained to give welfare rights advice. This period also saw the beginnings of work with members of St Martin's Church house groups, and the birth of the Writers Workshop and the Photo Workshop.

The cauldron was not only a period of powerful conflicting pressures. It was an intense period of thinking in which methods were worked out in theory and then tried out in practice, leading to further reflection, adaptation and refinement. The ALP workers learned through trial and error how to make good codifications. They began to learn the subtle skills of facilitating dialogue, finding decoding a powerful tool in spite of their initial awkwardness in using the method. They learned how important it was for participants in learning programmes to be able to withdraw from their normal situations of living, working and relaxing, into a quiet place where they could talk seriously about real issues. They learned how to translate and sometimes change Freire's language. Finally, they learned not to bite off more than they could chew, to be more realistic in limiting the scope of investigations, and more precise about the roles of participants at the various stages of the process.

Phase two: the bridge (1982–85)

The bridge covers the two-year extension of urban aid, plus a further six-month extension of funding by Lothian Regional Council. It is a process of crossing over from the initial period of experiment and innovation towards the later period of maturity. It is characterized by further clarification and refinement of the methods in a second major investigation, the coming to fruition of action outcomes from the first phase as autonomous organizations within ALP, the expansion of the role of the workers in the development of these groups, the growth of field work training, and the formation of the campaign group to find ways of securing the future of the project.

Two new investigations were undertaken, one into Health and Well-being, the other into people's awareness of the effects of New Technology on Society. The technology investigation was based on observation of the fascination people were showing with computers located temporarily in the ALP shop to give people hands-on experience. They were obsessed by the games and other programmes supplied and beginning to enquire about what computer courses were available.

The workers felt there was a need to widen people's interest in computers into an exploration of new technology and its impact on society. Interviews and group discussion revealed that many people's relationship to the higher forms of technology existed at the level of superstition. They had no direct experience of it and lacked the information to ask the right questions, but were willing to speculate about ways in which they felt technology was being used to control society. The gap between people's present grasp of high technology and the new knowledge they would need to master it was felt to be too wide for ALP to bridge, and this investigation ended after decoding. The computers were transferred to St Bride's Community Centre, where a computer workshop and basic computing skills courses were established.

The investigation into Health and Well-being had a firmer foundation in the project's past. It had been an aspect of the first investigation into Life in Gorgie Dalry. The Health Centre was a focal point in the area, and it seemed that many people had difficulty in relating to doctors. Some had horror stories to tell.

The ALP workers were anxious, however, not to limit the investigation to ill-health, the treatment of illness, and people's relationship to doctors.

They used the World Health Organization's idea of health as positive well-being, which is a broader concept. This allowed them to ask questions about the social circumstances that affect people's health for better or worse. It suggested the possibility of bringing people together who share some of the same life circumstances and whose health may therefore be affected in similar ways: workers, mothers at home with small children, the unemployed, and the elderly. Further, it allowed them to work with the contradictions in people's lives (e.g. motherhood and unemployment as both limiting and liberating), and to explore their strategies for survival as well as the ways in which they harm themselves or may be harmed by their circumstances. Finally it opened up the possibility of people taking action to improve their own health and sense of well-being.

Out of this investigation came the Living Memory Project for the elderly, and learning programmes called Women and Well-being and Health and Unemployment. These in turn led to action outcomes: the Loose-End Activity Centre for the unemployed and others around during the day, the Women's Health Group which began a further series of learning programmes on aspects of women's health, run by women themselves. At the same time a Well Woman Centre was established in St Bride's Community Centre. It grew out of a demonstration project in the Scottish Women's Health Fair in which one of the ALP workers was involved.

The creative efforts of the ALP workers and a growing number of residents were bearing fruit. The project had really taken root. The workers felt it was important to pass on what had been learned. The level of demand for training and consultation suggested that this role would grow. Residents who had experienced the effectiveness of ALP methods felt that there should be an ALP shop on the corner of every locality. But among policy makers in Scotland, the generic view of community education was still dominant, and what was seen as the specialist work of ALP did not square with this view.

Workers and ALP members were already meeting in a project co-ordinating group. With the end of urban aid funding in sight, this now became the campaign group. Residents wrote a case for the expansion of ALP and the employment of five workers on a permanent basis, which was widely circulated. It pointed up the achievements and future potential of the project and the need for resources to develop it. It argued that other areas should benefit from the experience. The idea of ALP becoming a fieldwork training unit was floated.

Throughout 1984 much energy was devoted to the campaign to establish ALP as a lasting presence. Reports were prepared for councillors and senior education officials. Delegations of ALP members addressed the regional education committee. The campaign group approached all those in high places who had been following the development of the project, and they responded with enthusiasm. Trainers and fieldwork practitioners were asked to say how their practice had been affected by contact with ALP. Residents were interviewed about their experience of the process. In response to invitations, the ALP workers led seminars or gave lectures on the methods in Aberdeen, Ayr, Bathgate, Dundee, Glasgow, Renfrew, Buxton, Oxford, Peterborough, and Nottingham.

A training conference on the adaptation of Freire's ideas in Gorgie Dalry, and their potential throughout the whole of the UK, attracted 50 practitioners from Scotland, England and Northern Ireland. The project was determined not to fade away. While efforts to secure ALP's future continued, Lothian Regional Council made arrangements for a temporary extension of funding. Finally in March 1985, ALP was established as part of the Community Education Service, with a staffing level of two education workers (one fewer than before), a secretary, and a dual remit for practice and training.

Some valuable lessons were learned during the bridge.

- It is useful to focus the scope of investigation more sharply, yet keep it broad enough for interconnections to be made.
- The relationship between reflection and action should be handled flexibly: action for health, for example, can take place within a learning programme, and need not await the action outcome stage.
- It's important to examine carefully the implications of proposals for action made by participants in a learning group. Are they feasible? Do the workers have the time and resources available to give the necessary support?
  Can they enlist the help of other professional workers in the area – and if so, can hand-over be successfully negotiated? Or can action outcomes be floated free of the project?
- It's important to maintain a balance in terms of staff time between innovative work, supportive work, and training. There were times during the bridge when the supportive role was taking up too much time and energy.

Phase three: maturity (1985–88)

The period of maturity has been characterized by increased confidence and flexibility on the part of the ALP workers. Having digested Freire's theory and methodology, and experimented with applications in a variety of settings, they are now able to focus in a more relaxed way on people's themes rather than on the mechanics of the process. Their more outward-looking approach is reflected in the frequency of collaborative projects during this period.

ALP members had played a key role in securing the future of the project. It seemed appropriate that this should be formally recognized and built into the structure. The ALP Association was now formed as a partnership between the paid workers and ALP participants. It is composed of representatives from each ALP group, plus co-opted members. Its tasks are to promote communication within the project between the different ALP groups; to support their development; to help organize the training of group leaders; to plan and assess the work of the project in partnership with the workers; to raise funds and organize social events; and to promote the project to the outside world.

With the opening of the Photo Workshop's darkroom at 4b Downfield Place, next door to the shop, the central role of photography in ALP has been confirmed and strengthened. Experienced Photo Workshop members tutor new members, and offer structured courses to groups of young, often unemployed, would-be photographers.

Establishment of the project gave a new lease of life to other organizations within ALP. The Writers Workshop expanded its programme of publications and performances. The Skills Exchange created a new system of swop nights and ran a series of short courses tutored by its own members.

With ALP's training role now formally recognized, it seemed appropriate to concentrate training efforts within Lothian. The Practitioners Skills Exchange was established, meeting on a monthly basis, and is still flourishing after three years. It brings together practitioners involved in leading learning groups in a variety of settings to share knowledge and experience and bring group wisdom to bear on problems members encounter in their work.

Two courses on ALP methods and their adaptation in other settings have been run for full-time Community Education Workers employed by Lothian Region. Throughout the period of maturity ALP workers have continued to respond to the still-growing volume of requests for individual consultations and to provide seminars and other training events throughout Scotland – and recently, for the first time, in the Republic of Ireland.

ALP has always responded to requests for information about educational opportunities available in the Region. In 1985/86 this role expanded when a pilot adult education information and advice service was run in the shop to help demonstrate the demand for such a service.

Another major investigation, called Parents and Authority, was begun. It grew out of previous work on disciplining young children, one of the issues which arose in the Women and Well-being programme. Since the start of the project, participants had been talking about their difficulties in relating to authority figures, and using their own authority. Within ALP itself, the issue of authority has been highlighed because of the demands the ALP process places on participants to take responsibility. Parenting provided a specific context for the exploration of this theme.

A group of mothers from the Women and Well-being programme recruited some of their friends and neighbours, including some fathers at home looking after children. Over 10 weeks participants explored their experiences of childhood and of being parents, interviewed partners and friends, built their own codifications, decoded them, and came up with a brief for a learning programme called Parenting in Different Cultures, expanding their groups to include immigrant parents. Out of this grew the Parents Centre, a permanent meeting place for local parents based in St Brides Community Centre.

Around the same time, the theme of authority was being explored in the context of football matches. A video of the Liverpool–Juventus game at the Heysel Stadium in Belgium was decoded, first by a group of ALP members and then by a group of young football players. Showing it had another purpose: to find out how to work with video as a means of codification. ALP workers had decided to explore television and its place in people's lives. With millions of people glued to their TV sets, a number of questions arise. How does watching TV affect other aspects of people's lives? What sort of learning is going on here? Would viewers, especially those who did not normally take part in ALP, be interested in decoding their favourite TV programmes?

The ALP staff and some experienced ALP members formed a group to learn everything they could about the production of television programmes in order to be able to co-ordinate a new series of programmes on popular TV, which has included SOAPS – the Inside Story, Mad about the Ads, and more recently Humour on the Box.

A new multi-disciplinary programme of courses for unemployed people, called Fresh Start, was launched, with elements of psychology, politics, maths, and creative writing. This involved the adaptation of the decoding process as a method of negotiating the curriculum with participants and briefing the specialist tutors. Fresh Start was offered in collaboration with Lothian Region's Careers Service who conducted interviews designed to help each participant work out where they might go after the course finished.

ALP is currently collaborating with Lothian Region's Adult Basic Education Unit to adapt Freirean methods to literacy work in a technologically advanced country where the manifestations and causes of limited literacy differ from those in Brazil. This has involved decoding discussions with students around their common concerns, followed by language work around key words used in the discussion. Both learning programmes – Living in Wester Hailes and People's Experience of Schooling in Wester Hailes – have involved people living in a large peripheral council housing scheme.

At the time of writing, another collaborative project is about to start, this time with Health Visitors based at the Springwell House Health Centre. The learning programme is called Living with a Toddler. The division of labour involved reflects the increasing flexibility of the process. The Health Visitor will host the session and act as observer and recorder. The ALP worker will co-ordinate the discussion, helping the group to identify the questions to be explored, and the Health Visitor will contribute her expert knowledge in response. The area Nursing Officer hopes that this collaboration will lead on to further involvement of health visiting staff in group work.

Finally, with the start of a new investigation called Living with Change in Gorgie Dalry, the work of the project has come full circle. The ALP workers are now returning to the streets where they first began knocking doors eight years ago, to ask residents how they feel about the changes that have taken place in the locality, the country at large, and the wider world.

Some of the lessons learned during this period of maturity can be summarized as follows:

- ALP workers have struggled to integrate the dimension of new knowledge more effectively into the process, for example, by working hand in glove with subject specialists, who act as consultants rather than visiting experts, throughout the programme.
- There has been an attempt to redress the balance between learning programmes and support for action outcomes, in favour of the

former, which is the major source of ALP's authority to be involved in adult education training.

- There are two distinct but closely intertwined tensions in ALP, between Freirean values and other values in our culture, and between structure and spontaneity. Both these tensions exist within ALP, perhaps less in the learning groups which are worker-led, and more in the action outcomes and workshops. A factor here is that once organizations are formed they recruit new members who have not been involved in creating them or establishing the principles on which they operate. Part of the ALP worker's supportive role is to carry out periodic reviews of the progress of each organization, in dialogue with its members, as a way of revivifying ALP values and orientation in the life of the group.

- The role of the ALP Association as a framework for the partnership between workers and members is problematic. The prime commitment of ALP participants is to their own learning group or autonomous organization. The development and promotion of the ALP project as a whole is a distinct task and can sometimes be experienced as too demanding of volunteers' time. There is also a question mark over whether it is appropriate for ALP members to be involved in planning and assessing the work of the full-time staff. For those who have been involved in the co-ordinating group of the Association, and have struggled with these tensions, the rewards have been a greater awareness of ALP values, its history, and its hopes for the future.

CHAPTER 2

Ideas and contexts

ALP is an ideas-intensive project set in a real historical context, so it is appropriate to give some account of those ideas and their origins. This chapter discusses changes in British society in the period leading up to the start of ALP, and aspects of the educational context, in particular the context of community education in Scotland. This is followed by an account of Paulo Freire's life and ideas, and the educational method he developed in Brazil and Chile. It is important not to give the impression that ALP simply represents the uprooting of Freire's ideas from their Latin American setting and their transplantation into the foreign soil of Gorgie Dalry. Translation and adaptation are more appropriate metaphors, suggesting the need for sensitivity to the meaning of words in different cultures, and to changes of environment in the widest sense.

The British context

British society from 1945 to 1970 was dominated by a political consensus which placed a high value on the social services provided by the welfare state, the nationalization of key sectors of the economy, and the expectation of full employment. It could be described as superficially secure, centralized and paternalistic. Living standards were rising steadily. The leading idea was welfarism. Yet to speak of ideas in any simple sense in the British context does not ring true. British governments in the 1950s and 1960s were pragmatic and empirical in outlook, adopting practical approaches to affairs based not on principles or long-term objectives but on short-term necessity. They distrusted theory, placing their faith in evidence which could be observed and quantified.

Attempts by the Heath government in the early 1970s to apply ideas of efficiency, profitability and labour flexibility to the British economy were defeated by trade union action. Strong centralized trade unionism was another feature of Britain during the period, but some of the intense discontent in British workplaces and communities during the 1960s and 1970s had more to do with people's rising aspirations than with the conflict between labour and capital.

Less ambivalent challenges to paternalism came from the community action, common ownership and women's liberation movements, which struggled to create decentralized, non-hierarchical and participatory ways of working. Yet alongside them occurred revivals of Trotskyist, Leninist and Stalinist versions of Marxism, which were fundamentally centralist in their ways of thinking and organizing.

As the 1970s advanced, the British ship of state was sliding bumpily downwards, with rising unemployment, increased cuts in services, and trade union protests, culminating in the winter of discontent in 1978. There was an atmosphere of loss of confidence and lack of direction.

In Scotland, meanwhile, the upsurge of popular nationalist feeling in the 1960s continued into the 1970s. Scottish MPs elected in 1974 kept up the pressure on Westminster to produce some kind of self-government. But the struggle to achieve an elected Assembly narrowly failed. The debacle of the 1979 referendum was followed, paradoxically, by an upsurge in the self-awareness of the Scots as Scots, developments in Scottish publishing and the arts, renewed interest in the languages of Scotland, and painstaking attempts to unify the self-government movement.

In the same year, the Conservative Party led by Margaret Thatcher came to power, inaugurating dramatic changes in British society from which Scotland has struggled to stay immune. Thatcherism has attacked welfarism and paternalism with the weapon of radical individualism, flying the banner of the free market, sound money, wealth creation, entrepreneurship, and tax cuts.

The fresh wind of popular capitalism has convinced millions of people that creating wealth, being self-interested, and looking after one's own is good, and that redistribution of wealth through the mechanism of taxation is bad.

The arrival of the Adult Learning Project, with its radical humanist orientation and its exploration of the twin themes of being-for-
self and being-for-others, coincided with the start of the Thatcher
era.

The education context

The qualifying examination at the end of primary school, intelli-
gence testing, and the division between senior and junior secondary
schools came increasingly under attack in the 1950s. The campaign
for comprehensivization increased in momentum and had effectively won the day by the end of the 1960s. In primary schooling
there was an emphasis on play, stimulating experiences, project
work, group work, expressiveness, creativity, and the whole child,
as opposed to the development of basic skills, discipline, and the
forcing of high attainment. Learning supplanted teaching in
educational theory.

Concern about evidence of correlations between levels of attainment and social class (and later race and gender) led to the adoption of
policies of positive discrimination, and gave further impetus to the
community schools movement, with its emphasis on relevance,
parental involvement and school-community links.

Even in their hour of triumph, however, the new orthodoxies
were being challenged, first from the political right, and later from
all sides. The Black Papers focused attention on the failure of
progressive education to deliver the goods in the development of
basic reading, writing and counting skills, and on the undermining
of the authority of the teacher. Educational researchers showed that
the empirical evidence did not always favour progressive methods.
Some Marxists attacked the notion of relevance and argued for high
quality traditional education as the best way forward for working
class children. A Labour Prime Minister called for a great debate on
education and opened it himself by arguing that schools were out of
touch with the needs of society, and especially with the needs of
industry. The Manpower Services Commission entered the field of
skills training for employment. The concept of education for capa-
bility was promoted. The venerable distinction between education
and training rebounded on the liberal establishment, as the pendulum swung towards training and away from education-as-an-end-
in-itself.

By the end of the 1970s, the emphasis was falling increasingly on utilitarian and instrumental justifications for education. Employability became the key word. Education and training either added value to the job seeker in the eyes of the potential employer, or its worth was questioned. Adult, further and higher education, too, began to feel the effects of the vocational assault. The value of non-applied research was questioned, and criteria of output and value for money were applied across the board.

The whole education sector has been shaken in its complacency, and the liberal humanist tradition, for the time being, is in disarray.

Community Education in Scotland

The Community Education Service in Scotland emerged in the years following the publication of the Alexander Report in 1975, which recommended the integration of adult education with youth and community work, the expansion of adult education, and the adoption of a community development approach.

There was a good deal of vagueness about what the term community education actually meant, but many took the view that the absence of a precise definition was functional, because it allowed for a wide range of possibilities. It was felt that community education should meet social as well as educational needs, value people's experience, be informal in style, respond to demand, work with everyone from the cradle to the grave, involve large numbers of people, reflect the shape and colour of local communities, and encourage voluntarism and self-help. There was an emphasis on leisure, enjoyment, expression, activity, freedom, and choice. The ethos of community education was to some extent a reaction to the ethos of education in formal settings like schools and further education colleges. The fact that there was no statutory obligation on regions to provide community education and no compulsion on people to use the service, also influenced the style of provision and the stance of the workers. The very notion of provision (as opposed to facilitating or enabling) was questioned.

The new service was launched at a time when the British economy was beginning to falter, and the first cuts in public services were being made. As a result, the 200 adult educators called for by Alexander to begin to give equal weight to that side of the community education equation were never appointed. The service continued to consist mainly of youth and community workers.

As the years went by, the all-inclusiveness of community education became the defining feature of its identity, expressed in the concepts of generic community education and the generalist worker. This resulted in the gradual devaluation of specialisms, including adult education and youth work. The generic worker was expected to have organizational and group work skills which could be used flexibly to meet the needs of a wide range of individuals and groups, with special attention being paid to the most disadvantaged.

Workers were mostly based in community centres, and expected to manage them with the help of local committees. They had to be jacks-of-all-trades, offering youth activities, leisure and recreation classes, community arts, local festivals, work with the physically and mentally handicapped, and lunch clubs for the elderly, with time left over for outreach work which might give rise to campaigns on local issues, or to issue-based adult education. In practice, they could not do all of these things, and tended to become organizers, with part-timers and volunteers running the specialized activities. The full-timers were seen as multipliers.

Although such a remit called for a range of skills, the individual workers were not supposed to present as professionals in their area, but to be informal, approachable, responsive, facilitators rather than teachers. They were to merge with the people, not stand apart as figures of authority.

It was into this context that ALP was born, at a time when the star of generic community education was rising, and the stock of specialism was low. Members of the South West Edinburgh Area Team, of which ALP became a part, were aware of the hopes that the project would create methods which would help them in the adult education aspects of their work. But some of them found Paulo Freire's ideas difficult to grasp, and could not see the relevance to their many tasks. Those who were interested and tried to apply the new ideas in their own work found it difficult to create the necessary time and space because of the pressure of their other roles. It is not surprising that the ALP workers were sometimes seen as privileged because they were able to concentrate on face to face work with learning groups.

The ALP workers, in their turn, were influenced by ideas prevalent in community education at the time, such as ease of access, worker availability, responsiveness, outreach, relevance, disadvantage, community, and community control. ALP has taken these ideas on board, but not uncritically.

Ease of *access* is reflected in the choice of a shop on the main road as the project's base. It is seen as important that the shop should be a welcoming environment, but there is an emphasis on intentional activity. It is not a place to hang around in.

ALP workers try to be *available* to listen to people. It has been said that if you have an idea for a project, ALP is a place where you can come and talk it through. But it is availability within the boundaries of the remit, which is to identify concerns which might become the basis of new learning programmes.

Availability implies listening and *responding* appropriately. This involves ALP workers in referral, educational information and advice giving, informal counselling, and simple human support. This is in addition to ALP's remit of initiating learning programmes and supporting action outcomes, and involves working in breadth as well as in depth.

Outreach implies meeting people in their own contexts. Once contact has been made, however, ALP has found it helpful to invite people to step out of their normal situations in order to engage in serious reflection.

The next idea is that of *relevance*. If community education is about valuing people's experience, and formal education is about gaining new knowledge, ALP tries to bridge that gap by founding the search for knowledge on an investigation of people's themes. Relevance can be limiting if it is interpreted as never going beyond where people are now.

The concept of *disadvantage* is based on empirical evidence of poverty and lack of uptake of public services by identifiable groups in society. The term is often applied to whole localities, by resource allocators concerned with the distribution of services. Urban aid funding is made available for work in such localities or with such groups, and this was true in the case of ALP. ALP itself, however, approaches the facts of disadvantage from a completely different angle. It aims to treat the whole area as a living code to be deciphered, and therefore seeks to work with a broad cross-section of residents. In the course of an investigation it will often focus on groups of residents who share similar life circumstances, but this is in order to maximize the potential for dialogue, learning and action. The contradictions and limits revealed contain positive as well as negative elements. They are a source of energy, enabling people to change and to act on their situation. In sum, ALP has a growth orientation, rather than a compensatory orientation.

Community is another key concept, at one level denoting locality, at another level encouraging people to generate and sustain networks of relationships, and the sense of a lively organic whole. In the locality sense, Gorgie Dalry is not one community but several. In the people sense, Gorgie Dalry has many networks and ALP has contributed to the process of generating new ones, bringing more people out of isolation. In the organic sense, a lively feeling of community exists in the area, energized by the activity of a whole range of organizations. It has to be said, however, that the themes identified in ALP groups have implications beyond the boundaries of locality and are shared by people living elsewhere. It is important to get the concept of community into perspective.

The other influential idea is *community control*, which was built into the urban aid application. The paid worker is seen as the servant of residents, a facilitator who, over a period of time, works him or herself out of a job. Over the years ALP has demonstrated that the role of the worker is also to lead, to innovate, and to train, and that the need for the full-timer does not go away. With the setting up of the ALP Association, community control has been superseded by the notion of partnership between paid workers and participants.

The life, ideas and methods of Paulo Freire

Life

Paulo Freire is a Brazilian, born in 1921 to middle class parents in the north-east port city of Recife. His family suffered severely during the great depression, and as a result Freire knew from his own experience what it meant to go to school hungry. At the age of 15 his academic performance was at a level two years behind that of his school-age group. The family's fortunes recovered sufficiently for him to complete his secondary education and enter the University of Recife, where he studied law, philosophy, and the psychology of language.

Freire was brought up as a Catholic, and after a crisis while at university, he returned to the practice of his faith. Freire's Catholicism, however, is not the variety which is familiar in Britain. He has been strongly influenced by the Christian personalist, Emmanuel Mounier, and above all by the theology of liberation.

Freire married Elza Oliveira in 1944 and together they have had five children. On completing his degree he worked briefly as a lawyer, then as a welfare official, then as director of the department of education and culture in the state of Pernambuco. It was here that he first began to develop his dialogical method of education. During the same period, he became involved in teaching the history and philosophy of education in the University of Recife, where he took his Ph.D. in 1959. He co-ordinated the adult education programme of the popular culture movement, setting up culture circles in slum areas and encouraging popular festivals and performances.

Brazil in the early 1960s was a remarkable country, culturally and politically, with flourishing socialist, communist, trade union and Christian movements. Eligibility to vote depended on the ability to read and write, and illiteracy was widespread. In 1961, the populist Joao Goulart was elected president. Popular culture movements and literacy campaigns grew in strength, particularly the basic education movement sponsored by the country's bishops.

It was at this point, in 1962, that Paulo Freire was appointed director of the new cultural extension service of the University of Recife. Later that year, Recife elected a left-wing mayor who further promoted the popular culture movement. The cultural extension service expanded its literacy campaign with assistance from the United States Agency for International Development (USAID). Freire was now organizing literacy programmes involving thousands of peasants in the north-east. By June 1963, his teams were working throughout the whole of Brazil. On 1 April 1964, the military intervened, taking over all levels of government. Freire was placed under house arrest, jailed for 70 days, and then sent into exile. It was in jail that he began writing his first book, *Education: The Practice of Freedom* (also published as *Education for Critical Consciousness*).

Freire went to Chile where he spent five years during the period of moderate Christian Democratic government headed by Eduardo Frei. He was again involved in literacy work, in the context of agrarian reform and rural technological development. Towards the end of the 1960s, he left Chile for the USA, where he taught at the University of Harvard. These were the years of black power, student militancy, community action, and protests against the draft to fight in Vietnam. These movements and their writings influenced Freire deeply. His first articles in English were now published, followed by his first English book, *Cultural Action for Freedom*. In 1972 came his most famous work, *Pedagogy of the Oppressed*.

In the early 1970s Freire went to Geneva as special educational consultant to the World Council of Churches, remaining there until the end of the decade. During this period he worked also with the Institute for Cultural Action, and was involved in helping to develop education programmes in newly independent African and Asian countries, forging particularly close links with Tanzania and Guinea-Bissau. In the early 1980s, Paulo Freire returned to Brazil, and he now lives and teaches in the city of Sao Paulo.

Writings

All of Paulo Freire's writings are important, but his best books are *Pedagogy of the Oppressed*, in which he discusses the post-literacy phase of education, *Cultural Action for Freedom*, which is about literacy, and *Education: the Practice of Freedom*, which gives valuable insights into the early development of his thought. Further details of Freire's publications are given in the select bibliography.

Although they will be moved and at times exhilarated, readers of Freire should not expect an easy ride. His work is full of polysyllabic words. He has been accused of using unnecessary jargon. Others suggest that he has been ill-served by his translators. The current enthusiasm for plain English is a justified reaction to the use of abstraction for obscurantist purposes. But abstraction can also illuminate. Freire's theory arises from careful reflection on practice, and from wide reading. He talks about practice in theoretical terms, and frequently gives examples. As he says, there is a constant flux and reflux from the abstract to the concrete and back again in his work.

For a succinct account of the man and his ideas, *Paulo Freire: His Life, Works and Thought* by Denis Collins is very helpful. For an understanding of his literacy work, including samples of his materials and an outline of his method, *Literacy in 30 Hours: Paulo Freire's Process in North-East Brazil* by Cynthia Brown is recommended. And for thoughts about education in schools and colleges *A Pedagogy for Liberation*, by Paulo Freire and Ira Shor, is stimulating.

Ideas

The influences on Freire's thought are many and varied: from Catholicism, Mounier, de Chardin, John 23rd, and liberation theology; from the Protestant tradition, Tillich and Buber; from phenomenology, Husserl; from philosophy and history, Hegel, Marx and Lukacs; from the Third World, Fanon and Memmi; from existentialism, Sartre; from psychoanalysis, Fromm; from politics, Guevara, Mao, and Nyerere. And there are many more. It might seem that Freire is an eclectic, a magpie stealing bits and pieces from here, there and everywhere, rather than an original thinker whose work is all of a piece. That would be the opposite of the truth. Freire has an ability to see, without envy, when another person has developed a concept, created a method, or offered a valuable insight, and to weave these elements into a congruent whole. In this sense, Freire – who does not claim originality and always gratefully acknowledges his sources – can be said to have synthesized an outlook which, in partial forms, has been available to human beings for centuries.

What is the essence of it? Where to start? Perhaps the simplest point of departure is the possibility of love. The avowal of feelings of love can make one appear ridiculous, as Freire recognizes. Love is an embarrassing and ambiguous word these days. Yet Freire writes frankly about his desire to help create a world in which it will be easier to love.

Freire is concerned with real people in their relations with each other and with the world. He is concerned above all, with those he calls the oppressed, the dispossessed, the colonized, the invaded, the marginalized – and therefore also with their oppressors. Freire believes that oppressed people are seen and treated as *objects*. He describes them as submerged in reality. This way-of-being-seen, this treatment, denies them their humanity. Instead, he believes that people should be seen and treated as *subjects* who can know and act on the world, whose task is to emerge from their condition of submergence, and to intervene in reality. For Freire, people are conscious beings who through their work transform the world, creating culture and history. Their vocation, he says, is to become more fully human.

Freire uses the word *culture* not in the familiar sense of high culture, nor in the sense of popular culture, but in the anthropological sense, which includes all the manifestations of a society, its work and its technology, its property relations and means of exchange, family and kinship, language, religion, institutions and values. He relies a great deal, both in his thinking and in his approach to education, on people coming to understand the distinction between culture and *nature*. Nature is everything that would be there without people: birds, fish, animals, rivers, the sea, the land, plants, trees, the sky. Culture (and history) is nature transformed by people, through their work. A grasp of this distinction, Freire believes, helps people to move from a fatalistic orientation in which they see themselves (and permit themselves to be treated) as objects, as parts of nature, to one of self-awareness and self-belief as makers of culture.

Connected with this view of the oppressed as objects is the recognition that they are beings-for-others. The objective of Freire's educational method is to help them in their struggle to become beings-for-self. In trying to understand these powerful twin themes, it is useful to consider the Talmudic saying:

> If I am not for myself, who will be for me?
> If I am for myself only, what am I?
> If not now – when?

Consciousness

A crucial feature of Freire's theory is his view of consciousness. To begin with, the word for *consciousness* in Latin-based languages has a wider meaning than it has in English, denoting not only awareness but also the idea of conscience, the capacity to make judgements and to have intentions. Freire sees consciousness not as a passive copy of the real, a vessel which the world enters and fills, but as active, intent upon the world, literally tending towards it. Human beings are capable not only of this intentional consciousness of the world, of others, and of self, but also – and he makes crucial use of this in his educational practice – they are capable of being conscious of their own previous consciousness. He refers both to perception of previous perception, and knowledge of previous knowledge.

Freire recognizes that human beings have different qualities of consciousness. He offers a metaphor from grammar: consciousness is either transitive or intransitive. A transitive verb is one whose action passes through into the object, and an intransitive verb is one in which it does not. The root meaning of transitivity (to go through or across) is close to the notion of activity as opposed to passivity, of doing as opposed to being done to, and to Freire's other metaphor of submergence and emergence.

Freire talks about an archaeology of consciousness, by which he means that human beings manifest different levels or stages of consciousness. Before describing these briefly, it is important to stress that Freire does not interpret them rigidly, for example he does not argue that people operate at one level of consciousness only. Everyone manifests different stages of consciousness not only at different times in their lives, but simultaneously. It is also important to point out that Freire does not believe that people can be totally intransitive, utterly lacking in *intentionality*. He speaks of semi-intransitivity, in which people know and act upon the world in a limited way in order to meet their biological needs only.

The first level of consciousness is magical consciousness. In it, people feel inferior to facts and events, which are experienced as having been commanded by a superior force or supernatural power, such as fate, destiny, or God.

As they develop their powers to understand their situation, and go beyond the simple biological sphere, they become transitive: there is a movement from disengagement to engagement; they begin to feel superior to facts and events. The first stage of transitivity is naive transitivity, characterized by a tendency to simplify problems, to go by appearances, and to accept received ideas rather than question them. This stage is characterized also by nostalgia for the past, and by a polemical rather than an investigative attitude. There is still an element of passivity. There is a tendency either to become reactionary (to fear the new), or to be into change for change's sake (to fear the old). Naive consciousness tends to see history as the deeds of great men or women, and communication as a form of imposition. Tomorrow is expected to be on the same pattern as today and yesterday. There is not yet an awareness of life or history as a process of becoming.

Naive consciousness can advance to the level of critical consciousness, or it can be deflected back to the level of fanaticism. Fanatical (or mythical) consciousness, in one account of Freire's ideas, is described as the second archaeological level, coming between magical and naive, but a careful reading of his work suggests rather that fanaticism is to be seen as a backward-deflection from naive consciousness. In fanaticized consciousness, people become dominated by a powerful myth (for example, that the Jews are the cause of the world's problems, or that coloured immigrants are the cause of Britain's problems) and act on the basis of emotion rather than reason. Believing themselves to be free, believing that they are making their own choices, they are in reality following prescriptions. They cease to reflect upon their situation, and become directed objects, a condition described by Freire as massification.

If this deflection into fanatical consciousness does not occur, people can proceed to full transitivity, which Freire describes as critical consciousness or critically transitive consciousness. It is not superficial, but seeks to go into, to go under, to under-stand, to go to the roots of, to unveil, to investigate, and is willing to test its findings. It is open to revision, seeks to avoid pre-conceptions, accepts responsibility, and is dialogical rather than polemical. Communication is seen as a collaborative search for truth.

Freire comments:

> the step from naive transitivity to critical transitivity does not occur automatically. It requires an active dialogical educational programme, concerned with social and political responsibility, and prepared to avoid the dangers of massification.

Words and themes

Another distinguishing feature of human consciousness is thought-language. Like the book of Genesis, Freire ascribes fundamental creative importance to language which is authentic. While Freire and the liberation theologians value parts of Marxism, accepting for instance its analysis of class and property relations ('that people are cheated in the sale of their labour'), they regard it as being of equal importance in the total picture of oppression that people are silenced, denied their voice, denied the right to speak. This differentiates Freire sharply from those versions of Marxism which locate language in the superstructure along with religion, law, and so on, which are seen as determined, in the last analysis, by the economic base.

For Freire, naming the world is the distinctively human activity, the core of being human. To exist, he says, is to name the world, to change it. To speak a true *word* is to transform the world. Some important qualifications must be made, however.

First, naming the world is not the privilege of the few, but the right of everyone. Secondly, you do not name the world on your own, but in dialogue with others. Thirdly, the word, or dialogue, does not consist of words alone. It is not just reflection, which he describes as mere blah, *verbalism*, empty words. The true word (or authentic *praxis*) includes work, and is conceived of as the simultaneity of reflection and action.

How, then, does Freire conceive of the world itself, and the relationship between consciousness and the world? First of all, the world is real: it is not an illusion. Freire speaks repeatedly of the empirical dimensions of reality, and of objective reality. As already mentioned, however, reality is seen not as a fixed given, but as a dialectical process of becoming. Where he parts company with empiricism, and where the empirical tradition seems impoverished by comparison, is in emphasizing that objective reality is known only through consciousness, through *subjectivity*. And Freire warns against dichotomizing subjectivity and *objectivity*. Human beings have to steer a course between the Charybdis of *subjectivism* or solipsism, and the Scylla of *objectivism*. Through their consciousness, using thought-language, in dialogue with each other, they unveil reality in a never-ending process of investigation which focuses not only on the objective situation, but on themselves as knowers. They have always to retain this recognition that they are investigating not just reality but their awareness of it and their relationship to it. In this respect, Freire's thinking overlaps with the outer/inner distinction in human relations thinking. It leads him to stress the importance of *intersubjectivity* and *co-intentionality*, and to the existence and importance of what he calls themes.

What Freire means by themes is difficult to explain, yet there is a sense in which everyone knows what themes are. Themes, he argues, are not things. They do not exist outside people. But they are not purely subjective, either. They exist in people's thinking, in their vision of the world, in what they hope for and fear, in what they strive to achieve or to avoid. Themes exist and are known in the relationship between people and the world. They exist at a range of spatial-temporal levels of scale, at epochal, world, inter-continental, continental, national, regional, district, local, family, interpersonal, and personal levels. They can exist simultaneously at various levels of scale, and in different eras: the twin themes of development and underdevelopment are a good example of this.

Education

The meaning of themes will become clearer when Freire's approach to education and the case studies of the work of ALP are discussed. Education, he says, is either for domestication or for liberation. It is either banking education or problem-posing education. It can be mixed but it cannot be neutral. Freire's insistence on the non-neutrality of education should be sharply distinguished from an educational orientation with an overt or covert alignment to a particular political party, theory, or set of policies, a stance Freire denounces in all its manifestations, whether on the right or the left. He opts, as we would by now expect, for an education based on conceiving people as subjects who can know and act upon the world in dialogue with each other. His educational means is to stimulate the development of critical thinking, and his objective is to contribute to the process whereby the oppressed and marginalized can make their entry onto the stage of history. This is characterized by a move from the status of spectator to that of actor, though Freire makes it clear that the quality of people's participation depends on their conscious-ness. He is not issuing a summons to mindless *activism*.

Literacy work

With this starting point, that people are subjects not objects, and the further assumption that they are interested in the situations in which they find themselves, Freire first of all dispenses with primers and rote-learning as a way of teaching people to read. He describes traditional primers as representing the nutritionist approach to education, in which empty vessels are fed with knowledge. Instead, Freire and his collaborators visit the area in which they intend to work, having first read about it in whatever secondary source material is available. They hold a public meeting, explain their intentions, ask for approval, and call for local volunteers to assist them. The team and their local co-investigators carry out a pro-gramme of observation and visits in the area, focusing on every important aspect of life: work, family, religion, social life, popular organizations, language. They report their findings to each other, gradually working towards a deepening understanding of the life of the area, its key situations, its contradictions, and its complex of themes.

In literacy work, one of their immediate objectives is to create a list of 16 or 17 *key words*. These are not chosen at random, but are existentially charged words, words representing important aspects of people's lives, which taken together include all the phonemes of the language. Some examples of the different lists created in various Brazilian communities are given on the following page:

List 1
Used in Cajueiro Sêco, a slum
in Recife

tijolo	brick
voto	vote
siri	crab
palha	straw
biscate	odd job
cinza	ashes
doença	illness
chafariz	fountain
máquina	machine (sewing)
emprêgo	employment
engenho	sugar mill
mangue	swamp
terra	land, soil
enxada	hoe
classe	class

List 2
Used in Tiriri, an agricultural
colony in the city of Cabo

tijolo	brick
voto	vote
roçado	manioc field
abacaxí	pineapple
cacimba	well
passa	raisin
feira	market
milho	corn flour
maniva	kind of manioc
planta	plant
lombriga	roundworm
engenho	sugar mill
guia	guide (for a blind person)
barracão	small store rooms near market place
charque	dried meat
cozinha sal	kitchen salt

List 3
Used in Maceio, a city on the sea

tijolo	brick
voto	vote
casamento	wedding
carroça	cart
peixe	fish
jangada	fishing boat
balança	scale for weighing fish
Brasil	Brazil
máquina	machine (sewing)
farinha	flour
coco	coconut
fome	hunger
comida	food
sindicato	union
trabalho	work
limpeza	cleanliness

List 4
Used in the state of Rio, a rural area
and satellite of the city of Rio de
Janeiro

favela	slum
chuva	rain
arado	plough
terreno	plot of land
comida	food
batuque	popular dance with African rhythms
poço	well
bicicleta	bicycle
trabalho	work
salário	salary
profissão	profession
govêrno	government
mangue	swamp
engenho	sugar mill
enrada	hoe
tijolo	brick
riqueza	riches, wealth

Codifications and decoding

Simultaneously the investigators prepare a series of codifications to accompany the chosen key words. Codifications, at the literacy level, are visual representations of significant situations in the lives of people in the area. They usually take the form of sketches or photographs. The elements in a codification, the relations of these elements to each other, to the whole picture, and to the situation represented, are arranged so as to embody important themes and contradictions in the lives of the people. Codifications, according to Freire, need to have the following characteristics: they must represent familiar and easily recognizable situations; they must not be too explicit or too enigmatic – neither making propaganda nor seeming like a puzzle; they should offer various decoding possibilities; they should be arranged in a thematic fan or sequence, with one theme opening onto another; all the codifications in a sequence should make up a totality, and contain what he calls the inclusive contradictions, by which he means those key contradictions of the area which recur in various aspects of its life; and (a variation added in Chile) codifications should relate to felt needs, in order to stimulate initial engagement.

Freire regards it as desirable that at least 10% of the inhabitants of the area take part in the *culture circles* which are formed, with a maximum of 20 people in each circle. The culture circle meeting is co-ordinated by one of the team, and happens like this: the participants begin to talk about the picture, first at the level of describing what is in it. Gradually they go deeper, discussing how elements in the picture relate to each other or to the whole, or to some aspect of the real life situation portrayed, focusing perhaps for a time on how one participant sees an aspect of the picture or of the reality. There is a flux and reflux from part to whole, and from representation to reality.

The role of the co-ordinator is to encourage this process of description by asking questions, listening, and sometimes challenging. The challenge is directed not to the person speaking but to the statement made, posing or re-presenting to the whole group as a problem to be tackled. What do you mean by that? Why is that important? Freire calls this the problematizing or *problem-posing* role of the co-ordinator. This process of description shading into reflection, of dialogue with elements of analysis and synthesis, of abstraction and return to the concrete, is called decoding. In it, participants make explicit their real consciousness. They exteriorize their themes. To put it in terms more familiar in English, they express how they see the world and live in it. Further, they perceive their previous perceptions, an experience which Freire believes stimulates new perceptions. This is the beginning of the process he calls *conscientization*, the stimulation of critical consciousness.

A wider interpretation of what Freire means by conscientization is given by Cynthia Brown in *Literacy in 30 Hours*:

> conscientization is a process in which people are encouraged to analyse their reality, to become more aware of the constraints on their lives, and to take action to transform their situation.

In the literacy process, an appropriate word from the list is now inserted into the picture. Having discussed the situation, the participants now see the familiar word, one they know how to say but may not know how to write. The co-ordinator introduces it, invites them to say it several times, and then breaks it down into syllables. Participants are invited to say each syllable in turn. The co-ordinator now introduces a discovery card which shows each syllable of the word in a sequence or family of syllables based on the five vowel sounds. Take the word tijolo, meaning brick. The discovery card looks like this:

ta	te	ti	to	tu
ja	je	ji	jo	ju
la	le	li	lo	lu

Participants are invited to read each family of syllables several times. Then they are encouraged to make their own words by combining syllables any way they like. They quickly get the idea and begin making words, some of which are not words actually used by people, and some of which are. A member of one of Freire's culture circles called the non-words dead words, and the actual words thinking words.

It is claimed that participants learn to read and write in this way very quickly and with great enthusiasm. The essence of it as an approach to education is clear: existentially charged words, relating to important situations; description shading into analysis; movement from representation to reality, and from part to whole; perception of previous perception; with the learners actively and reflectively involved throughout and literally creating their own words.

Freire uses the term generative word to refer to the key words the team of co-investigators has chosen. They are generative because other words can be made out of them by means of the process described above, and because they generate discussion and reflection, leading in turn to other words and themes.

Post-literacy work

In post-literacy work, the process is very similar, the main difference being that the concept of generative word is replaced by the concept of generative theme, with the adult educators and their local co-investigators carrying out an investigation into what Freire calls the people's thematic universe, or meaningful thematics.

The process of codification of themes is similar to the one that has just been outlined, with the obvious difference that key words are not inserted into the codifications. Another difference is that the codification itself need not be visual, although it can be. It can consist of written extracts or taperecorded interviews, with photographs of the authors in either case, magazine or newspaper articles, book chapters, slides, filmstrips or videotapes, or combinations of these.

The decoding discussions take place in thematic investigation circles, and these are attended by two further specialists whose task is to observe and note significant reactions on the part of participants. In *Pedagogy of the Oppressed*, Freire gives an illuminating example of the kind of discussion that can occur in a thematic investigation circle:

> In one of the thematic investigations carried out in Santiago, a group of tenement residents discussed a scene showing a drunk man walking on the street and three young men conversing on the corner. The group participants commented that 'the only one there who is productive and useful to his country is the souse who is returning home after working all day for low wages and who is worried about his family because he can't take care of their needs. He is the only worker. He is a decent worker and a souse like us.'
>
> The investigator had intended to study aspects of alcoholism. He probably would not have elicited the above responses if he had presented the participants with a questionnaire he had elaborated himself. If asked directly, they might even have denied ever taking a drink themselves. But in their comments on the codification of an existential situation they could recognize, and in which

they could recognize themselves, they said what they really felt.

There are two important aspects to these declarations. On the one hand, they verbalize the connection between earning low wages, feeling exploited, and getting drunk – getting drunk as a flight from reality, as an attempt to overcome the frustration of inaction, as an ultimately self-destructive solution. On the other hand, they manifest the need to rate the drunkard highly. He is the 'only one useful to his country, because he works, while the others only gab'. After praising the drunkard, the participants then identify themselves with him, as workers who also drink – 'decent workers'.

The last stage of the investigation is a study of the findings of the decoding sessions, by an interdisciplinary team of co-investigators and other specialists. A list of explicit and implicit themes is made, and classified according to the different social sciences, though it is expected that several themes will figure in more than one classification. Each specialist then prepares a plan for a sequence of learning units, and when these have been discussed once more by the interdisciplinary team, a body of learning materials is prepared, and the next stage of the programme is implemented.

Freire is not opposed to experts, nor engaged in undermining their authority, but he does wish to ensure that their knowledge is used dialogically. That is why they are presented as human makers of culture, like the other members of the circle, and not as gods. The picture of the expert shows participants that he or she is another person, like themselves.

Limit situations

There is one further stage in Freire's educational process, though it is unclear from his work if the educators themselves are involved in it. In the course of investigating the contradictions contained in their themes, participants come up against *limit situations* in their real circumstances. These can perhaps best be described as blocks to their further humanization. At first these limits are experienced as insuperable boundaries which cannot be overcome. As the process of conscientization deepens and confidence grows, however, they are seen no longer as the limits of what is possible, but the points at which new possibilities begin. Beyond them lies a domain of untested feasibility. These limit situations evoke from participants what Freire calls limit acts. This is a reference to the political or action-follow-up implications of the educational work. The objective of conscientization is fundamental democratization, to be achieved, Freire believed, in the Brazilian context of the early 1960s, by participation in peasants' and community associations, trade unions, co-operatives, political parties, and so on. Before embarking on his educational work, Freire states that he seeks a promise of no political interference from governmental authorities, and advises them in general terms as to the likely outcomes of the educational programmes. His orientation, it should be said again, is not anti-authority: on the contrary he argues that authority should be on the side of freedom.

It is not clear whether Freire sees limit situations as belonging to the external world only, or whether he recognizes that there are also inner barriers which people need to confront and transcend. The ALP workers would argue that it can be both, and that the dialectic of inner and outer worlds and their respective limit situations is complex. More work needs to be done in developing this area of Freire's theory and method.

Note of acknowledgement

In addition to Paulo Freire's own books and articles, the author has drawn on the work of Denis Collins and Cynthia Brown in writing this section. The interpretation is his own.

CHAPTER 3

Investigations and learning programmes: case studies

In this chapter a selection of the main investigations and learning programmes are presented, in the following order:

1. *Investigation: Living in Gorgie Dalry*

Leading to learning programmes: *The Family Today* (2 groups)
You and the School (2 groups)
On Being Scottish (2 groups)

2. *Investigation: Health and Well-being*

Leading to learning programmes: *Health on the Dole* (1 group)
Women and Well-being (3 groups)

3. *Investigation: Parents and Authority*

Leading to learning programme: *Parents, Children & Authority: how Britain compares with other countries (2 groups)*

The aims of these case studies are:

- To give the reader a sense of what investigation, decoding, and taking part in learning programmes actually feels like for participants and for co-ordinators.
- To illustrate the process, and by demonstrating some of the

difficulties encountered and the adaptations made, to trace its development.

- To give adult education fieldworkers and trainers enough examples of methods and responses at each stage to enable them to apply or adapt the process in their own work.

Efforts have been made to standardize the presentation of case studies and to signpost each stage in the process clearly. But every investigation and learning programme is unique structurally, experientially and thematically. The styles of co-ordinators, recorders and *resource persons* vary. These factors are reflected in the different shape and texture of each case study.

Any experience of dialogue in a learning group includes material which seems to add nothing fresh, although it may be of great importance to the contributor. There is fluctuation from high to low intensity, and from relative confusion to clarity. Co-ordinators and members alike can miss important themes, and even deviate temporarily from the task. Readers should not look for perfection. In the selections made we have sought to give a balanced impression.

Readers are referred to the ALP tree on page 16 for the place of each investigation and learning programme in the overall development of the project, and to the diagram of the stages of the ALP process on page 7. Details of the number and type of participants involved are given in the statistical section at the end of the book.

1. Investigation: living in Gorgie Dalry

Stage of process	Text	Duration	Numbers involved
finding co-investigators	door knocking, public meetings	6 weeks	400 houses 17 at meeting
co-investigation	interviews, visits of observation, weekly meetings	16 weeks	12
decoding	family, wider context, school, work, women, media, Scottish identity	9 weeks	30
learning programmes	Family Today, You and the School, On Being Scottish	10 weeks	62

5. An ALP learning group

This case study has been selected because it is ALP's first investigation. In its length and breadth, it demonstrates three struggles: to get a new project off the ground; to comprehend the area in its totality; and to create a new method of working.

Finding co-investigators

A major issue in finding volunteer helpers in adult education and community work is whether to go for people who are already active in community organizations, or to recruit from among uninvolved residents. It is possible to opt for one strategy or the other, or to use a mixture of both. The advantage of going for existing activists is that you gain the benefit of their networks of contacts, their knowledge of the area and its problems, and the support of their organizations. The disadvantage is that you may be excessively influenced by their way of seeing the life of the area, and that their involvement may inhibit other residents from taking part. In the case of ALP, a decision was taken at the outset to recruit co-investigators from the whole population of the area, with an emphasis on those who were not yet involved.

The ALP workers therefore opted for a door-knocking strategy. They knocked on a total of 400 doors in the streets around the shop, and organized two follow-up public meetings. They found that early evening was the best time to get people in. Some opened the door a crack, and closed it again quickly. Others asked if the workers belonged to a religious organization. Some men, hearing the word community, called their wives. Those who picked up on the word education joked about being too old to learn. A few were insulted by the invitation. *They* didn't need educating, but some of their neighbours *did*. On a number of occasions the ALP workers were invited in and given the opportunity to explain the project. Twelve people volunteered to become co-investigators: three young mothers, three elderly women, three young men with jobs, and three young women, one with a job and two who were unemployed. The group included long-term residents and incomers. They all liked the area but were mostly not involved in local organizations.

Co-investigation

In the process of getting to know each other, members explored personal themes, such as changes in the area, psychological distance from their neighbours, fear of strangers, violence and break-ins, and their feelings of isolation. On the other hand they spoke of the friendliness of the area, and its potential for co-operation.

To help members overcome their diffidence about the task of interviewing other residents and observing moments of life in the area, the ALP workers discussed the sort of questions they might ask, and what to look for. For observing moments, they emphasized the need to describe any situation in terms of *where* it was, *who* was taking part, *what* they were talking about, and *why*; to give an account of the content of conversations and of the interactions taking place; and to note people's personal style and behaviour. For interviewing, the importance of open questions was stressed, some prepared in advance, others suggesting themselves during the flow of conversation; and of noting the actual words used by interviewees. People were encouraged to make written notes, or use a taperecorder.

Visits were made to places where people come together: the laundrette, local pubs, a committee meeting of the city farm group, the baby clinic at the health centre, the primary school, the day centre for the elderly, a cafe, the community centre, the bingo hall, a church, a playgroup, the supermarket, small shops, and a football match. Interviews were with pensioners, young mothers, a worker about to be made redundant, a political activist, and relatives and neighbours of the co-investigators.

Participants reported back weekly at co-investigators meetings, sharing each other's findings and beginning to identify themes and contradictions, such as insiders' and outsiders' views of the area, the need to protect one's privacy versus the need for the company of others, the effect TV has of limiting communication with others, the division in society between the doers and those who are done unto, and the theme of being Scottish. There were tensions in the group between long-term residents and incomers, old and young, and those who were around in the area during the day and those who appeared in the evening.

Building codifications

Once the co-investigators had clarified the emerging themes and contradictions, and discussed how to illustrate them, the ALP workers briefed the artist and the photographers whose task was to make the codifications.

Recruiting for decoding

Recruiting people to join decoding discussions coincided with the move into the ALP Shop. An open day was held, with blown-up photographs and brightly coloured posters in the windows, children walking on stilts on the pavement outside, distributing leaflets, and talking to people in the street. The workers also visited community groups, requesting activists to pass the word through their own networks, and the co-investigators invited their relatives and friends. A difficulty at this stage was how to explain the process of decoding, which neither ALP workers nor residents had yet experienced! Nevertheless, 30 people joined the three decoding groups which met weekly for seven weeks, either during the day or in the evening.

Decoding

The first meeting addressed the theme of the isolation of individuals in the community, relationships with neighbours and the world outside the home. The codifications used were two drawings, one of a couple in a flat with the busy streets of Gorgie Dalry in the background, the other a cross-section of different households on a common stair.

Home was seen as a refuge from the pressures of work and the physical environment:

> You spend a lot of time playing with your child indoors. There's not much space in the flat, but it's dangerous outside because of traffic. It's cosier and cheaper to stay at home. You can be yourself, keep yourself to yourself. You only meet your neighbours on the stair when there's a common problem.

The second meeting was called Gorgie Dalry in context. It addressed the theme of how people see themselves and the area, and how they feel they are seen by outsiders. The codifications included an aerial view of Gorgie Dalry in the wider setting of the west end of the city, and photos of streets of tenements, shops and small factories, with some of the housing undergoing rehabilitation, cars parked along both sides of the road, and children playing in the street. What emerged in discussion was a view of the relationship between Gorgie Dalry and the west end as a class division between workers and employers. People in Gorgie Dalry were seen as the artisans, the ones who get their hands dirty,

> wee sort of homey people, crouched down, not walking tall.

How would a vandriver going through the area see it? As broken down, busy, grimy, decayed, depressed, reminding people of Glasgow and Dundee. People from the west end shop in Dalry Road. They'd describe it as a good shopping area, but they wouldn't consider living there.

A connected theme was that of a community under pressure: kids being harassed by older people; new neighbours moving in who didn't share your values; a warehouse being built on precious spare ground instead of a playpark: and rehabilitation seen as a cause of upheaval and financial hardship.

The third meeting was on the theme of schooling. The codifications used were a drawing of mothers at the school gate watching the

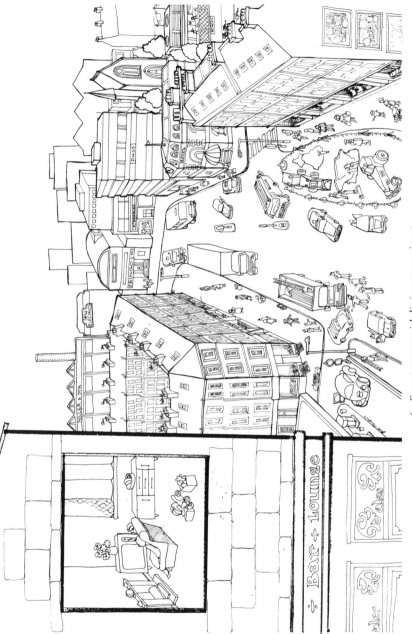

6. Street scene with living room inset

lines of children go in, and a drawing of a traditional classroom and an informal classroom side by side. Here are some of the questions used:

> What do children learn at school?
> Why are they at school?
> What do parents teach their children?
> What is the teacher contributing, in the traditional classroom, and in the informal classroom?
> What are the children contributing to each other's learning?

A complex picture emerged from the discussions. Home and school were seen as two different worlds. The school gate was a barrier. What went on in school was the teachers' business. Parents felt they couldn't be more involved while they were out at work, even if they wanted to. The traditional classroom was seen as representing their own schooling. The teacher talked and the children sat and listened. It was disciplined and orderly.

Participants approved of corporal punishment, but disapproved of its effect, which was to make them pay attention out of fear rather than interest. Nevertheless, they still believed that the teacher's job was to make their children listen. Good children paid attention and put up with it. Speaking out was seen as challenging the teacher's authority and showing disrespect.

On the whole, participants did not favour informal methods, though they recognized that their children were happier at school than they had been.

> The children are doing everything. The teacher's just observing. Classrooms are brighter than they were 20 years ago. It's called do-it-yourself learning. I think there's too much going on for the kids to concentrate. Where does the teacher actually teach English or Maths in that situation?

Some participants were aware that their view of themselves had been negatively affected by schooling.

> There are thousands of people who right down, hidden, submerged, believe that they're quite smart, but there's just layer upon layer of stuff telling them that they're not as valuable to society as other people. If you get it stuffed up your nose for years and years you believe it eventually.

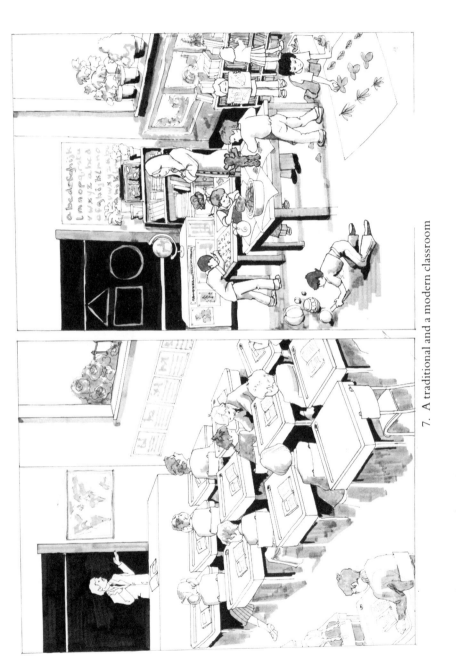

7. A traditional and a modern classroom

Exploring the question of whether an effective alternative to traditional schooling could be created, one participant commented:

> The greatest form of education is being able to cope with yourself.

In the fourth week the groups looked at work, using photographs of Ferranti workers: draughtsmen, a woman electronic component assembler, and a typist. An extract from an interview with a woman shop steward was also used.

> What is this worker doing?
> How much skill is involved?
> What is she thinking about?
> How much say does he have over how he does his job?
> How does he relate to his peers and those above and below him?
> How much control do *you* feel you have in your work?
> How does it fit in with the rest of your life?

Most participants felt that they were cogs in the wheel, cut off from other workers, having only negative power – to skive, to strike, to commit minor acts of sabotage. Work was often experienced as being regimented, like school. Workers were divided among themselves, for example manual workers and office staff. Even the power of shop stewards was limited. Most participants limited their investment in work. What was important in life happened outside:

> As soon as I walk out that door at 6.15, that's me finished with it. I wouldn't cry too hard if I lost my job, but I'd have to find something else to do or I'd just go down the tubes. As it is now you think: 'Friday – great'. You go in on Monday shattered, totally wrecked.

In the fifth week the groups looked at women as home-makers and workers. The codifications included photographs of a family walking in the streets, a mother at home feeding her child, women standing at the school gate, a woman teacher, and girls in a typing pool. Questions included:

> What does a woman get out of being at home?
> What does she miss out on?
> What do men contribute to family life?

8. An electronic component assembler

Women who left work to bring up children were felt to have exchanged one routine for another, but as one woman said:

at least she'll be calling the shots.

The job of bringing up a child was considered important in itself. The main drawback was the isolation.

9. Mothers outside the school gate

There's a young girl up the stairs from me, her baby's two months old. She's finding it hard to adjust. She was a nurse. She misses meeting her friends at work. She's tired. They don't have the money to go out. She's having a lonely time. She's the only mother with a baby on the stair. There's a young couple both out working, two elderly women on their own, an empty house, and myself with teenage children. She hasn't got to know all the neighbours yet. Her friends live out of the district. The baby's too small for a mother and toddler group.

The life of these women revolved around children. Discussing the picture of mothers waiting outside the school gate, one participant said:

They're wondering if their children are ever going to appear. Is my kid going to be vomited out the door this time, or is he lost in the mechanics? (laughter)

The picture of the young family walking along Dalry Road evoked powerful responses, particularly about father, who was seen

10. Family in the street

as a shadowy, peripheral figure. He kept the family fed and clothed, but didn't have a central role in bringing up the children. One participant remembered his own father:

> Your dad comes home at 5.30 knackered, gets something to eat, sits down and watches TV or goes out for a pint with his mates. Then you don't see him because he's up early in the morning. You're always glad to see him. It was a big thing if your father came down to play football with you.

Women's work was seen as low-paid and low in status, often involving caring, and linked to the role of women as mothers.

The next session was about how the world outside people's personal experience is mediated to them through TV, newspapers and street advertising. Codifications used were a drawing of a street scene outside the ALP Shop, with the advertisements picked out in colour and a sketch of a family at home watching TV. Among themes expressed were anger at the lack of restriction of advertising in an area like Gorgie Dalry, compared to one of Edinburgh's

11. After work – in the pub

conservation areas. People commented on the fact that most of the advertisements were for cigarettes and drink.

TV was seen as affecting every aspect of life:

> Everything's geared to the programme people want to watch. If I didn't watch telly, I'd talk a lot more, do a lot more, meet people more.

TV's role as childminder was recognized, limiting the relationship between mother and child but freeing her up to do other things. People suspected the media's role as information-giver:

> It's difficult to decide what's a fact and what's opinion on TV or the newspapers. If something is reported in the paper that you know about personally, it can read very peculiarly.

This resident, a civil servant, had recently taken part in a strike, and found it difficult to recognize his experience in the media coverage of it.

The last session was about Scottish identity, and used a photograph of Scottish fans invading the pitch at Wembley in 1977, after

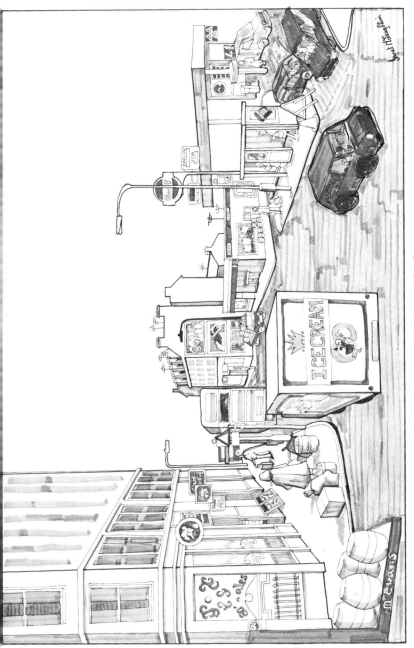

12. View from the ALP shop with adverts

their team had beaten England at football. As in all decoding sessions, the ALP workers had prepared a sequence of open questions at three different levels.

Descriptive	1. What do you see in the photograph?
	2. What is this event?
	3. What is happening?
Affective	1. How do the people in the photograph feel?
	2. How do they feel about each other?
	3. Who is this man shaking his fist at? What might he be saying?
	4. Have you ever felt like that? What were the circumstances?
Interpretative/ analytical	1. What does the photograph tell you about the relations between Scotland and England?
	2. What is it about the lives of these people that makes them behave in this way?
	3. What has it got to do with being Scottish?

Prepared questions are not used rigidly. The co-ordinator follows where the group leads, sometimes omitting questions, and always forming supplementary questions from contributions by participants.

The Scots were seen as being at war with the English, and the English as ignorant of the Scots. The difference was seen as a class difference, with the Scots as the working class. The English were also seen as being better at dealing with authority figures. The Scots saw themselves as born losers, not taken seriously by the English. Likewise they saw Scottish institutions as having no real power. Participants felt the Scots were perceived as being like exuberant children who were beyond parental control. One woman, who had just returned from a visit to a relative in the United States, spoke about the American Indians who were employed as ranch hands, seen as the town drunks, did nothing, got treated like children, and weren't expected to be too intelligent. She wondered if that was how the English saw the Scots.

This codification evokes a strong response no matter who it is used with. The comments of Scottish participants are always ambivalent,

13. Scottish football fans at Wembley, 1977

reflecting feelings of both shame and pride about their Scottish identity.

Issues arising from decoding

During this first series of decoding sessions, important issues about the approach came up. The unfamiliarity of the method made some people initially suspicious. Being asked questions reminded them of their schooldays, when there was always a right or wrong answer. It took people time to realize that the co-ordinator was trying to ask open questions which didn't have a correct answer implied in them. Sometimes, too, the open questions were seen as too simple, like Mickey-Mouse questions.

In their newness to the method, the co-ordinators occasionally stuck too rigidly to the pre-planned framework of questions. They gradually learned to loosen up and find questions appropriate to the themes actually emerging in the discussion.

Each group consisted of a mixture of people with different

experiences, not all of whom could identify with the situation represented in each codification. Also, workers sometimes introduced too many codifications into a single meeting. And they were still wrestling with the question: What makes a good codification?

Another problem, for co-ordinator and members alike, was people's lack of practice in dialogue. They were used to free-flowing discussion but unfamiliar with a structured process in which they were encouraged to build on each other's contributions. The idea that the purpose of the discussion was to produce themes which would form the basis of later learning programmes was unfamiliar too. An underlying problem here was the lack of value people placed on their own experience and opinions. They were surprised and pleased to have their views taken seriously.

There was some initial suspicion of the role of the observer/recorder, who was seen as a sort of psychologist. As they began to do a job for the group and it became clear that their observations were tentative and could be challenged, this suspicion dissolved.

Finally, the ALP workers took too much responsibility for analysing the contributions of participants and naming emerging themes. Later in the development of the process, this task was shared with members of the decoding groups.

Building the curriculum

The decoding discussions were taperecorded. The workers highlighted key statements and began to name the emerging themes. Copies were sent to participants, and a one-day workshop was set up with a view to organizing the statements into categories, and identifying the underlying themes. These were *barriers to communication, polarization between groups in society, the individual's relationship to authority*, and *power and powerlessness*. It was recognized that they overlapped with each other, and a number of statements were put in more than one category. The ALP workers pointed out that the first three could be regarded as sub-themes of the last: *power and powerlessness*.

The task now was to create interdisciplinary learning programmes. Experts from such disciplines as psychology, sociology, history and politics were invited to comment on the material produced.

Learning programmes

After consultation it was decided to focus on three contexts in which the theme of power and powerlessness had been identified as important. Three learning programmes were built: *The Family Today*, *You and the School*, and *On Being Scottish*. A broad sequence for each meeting was agreed: saying your own word, presentation by an expert, and dialogue. Our intention here was to reverse normal practice, where the expert makes a presentation and a period is left at the end for questions. Our sequence was based on a recognition that people have their own experience and knowledge to contribute, and their own lines of enquiry to pursue.

The expert would be the guest of the group, called in to add his or her specialist knowledge to the pool and engage in a dialogue with other participants.

Just as each session or meeting started from personal experience and moved outwards from it, so each programme, and all three programmes taken together, had a similar movement. The aim was to link personal experience with broader social phenomena, moving backwards and forwards between the personal and the political, creating opportunities for participants to recognize how the one influences the other.

The three programmes represented different levels of reality. The Family Today was concerned with the private world, You and the School with an interface between the private world and the public world at the local level, and On Being Scottish with national identity, and people's place in the wider world. All three learning programmes ran simultaneously, for six weekly meetings plus a review meeting. Each programme was run twice, for example mornings and evenings, to give as many people as possible a chance to join. Over 60 people enrolled. Below, a brief summary of the ground covered in each session is given. Resource persons included a child psychologist, a community minister, a sociologist, a tenant, a Housing Association official, a doctor, a member of a commune, two teachers, a community education officer, a politics tutor and a theologian.

The Family Today

1. Children develop authority and grow into responsible adults by challenging the values and authority of their parents. Good

enough families provide the conditions for each member to grow and change.

2. Women now have control of contraception and men are no longer the sole breadwinners. But women are still assumed to be responsible for childcare. Real changes in the division of labour between men and women are still limited.

3. The nuclear family developed to meet the needs of industrial society, when home life and work became split off from one another. Can it meet all the needs of its members for deeper relationships? What form will the family take in the aftermath of the impact of new technology?

4. Can families influence the physical environment in which they live? Should tenants be encouraged to become involved in the process of decision-making within Housing Associations, or are they right in thinking that the real decisions are made elsewhere?

5. Can families influence the health care they receive? Should doctors be more concerned with the conditions which cause ill-health? Can people learn to take more responsibility for their own health? Do we need to see doctors as all-powerful?

6. How does living in a commune compare with living in a nuclear family? There's a tension between the need for privacy and the need for support and company. The balance between the two varies in different parts of the world.

You and the School

1. Does school meet the needs of children struggling to develop their own authority and become responsible adults?

2. What should secondary schools educate children for? Formal and informal methods of education: which methods serve which aims? What values are implicit in the different methods?

3. A day in the life of a school. The potential for power-sharing between parents, teachers, pupils and government.

4. How are the subjects that make up the curriculum chosen?

5. Societies pass on their values and skills through their education systems. Four other systems of education presented and discussed. Changes we would like to see in our own.

6. Differences between the Steiner system of education and the state system. Should government finance alternatives?

On Being Scottish

1. The process by which we develop our sense of identity. Scotland as a collection of tribes. The Scots as locked in adolescence, challenging authority, and blaming the authority outside themselves.
2. How Scotland gradually lost its identity after the union of parliaments. How can the Scots develop a strong sense of national identity *and* retain a sense of themselves as part of the world community?
3. How the Church contributed to Scottish identity. The democratic forces behind the rise of Calvinism. The undemocratic notion of the elect. The division into religious tribes. Church membership as giving a sense of belonging but also alienating us from others.
4. Working-class experience from 1800 to the present. Scotland's working-class image. Vibrant poets, novelists and playwrights. Lack of cohesion and leadership in Scotland.
5. The arguments for and against a Scottish Assembly. Why so many Scots voted 'no' in the referendum. Underlying fear of change.
6. A look at the meaning of culture. Can we help create it as well as being influenced by it?

Action outcomes

From among the people following the three learning programmes, a new group was formed to identify immediate concerns which might become the focus of local action. These included neglected gardens, the overgrown canal, traffic danger to children, conflicts among neighbours, the closure of local factories, redundancy, and cuts in the resources available for local playgroups and nursery schools. Case studies of two of the action outcomes which developed are presented in Chapter 4.

Issues arising from learning programmes

- By choosing to focus on *contexts* in curriculum building, there was some loss of clear focus on *themes*.
- The ALP workers were still inexperienced at using subject experts to help them build interdisciplinary learning programmes.

- It was difficult to integrate the contributions of each discipline in the learning programmes. They tended to become multidisciplinary rather than interdisciplinary.
- Resource people found it unsatisfying to make their contribution in one session only.
- Several resource people found it hard to dialogue with participants, and tended to hog the airwaves.

2. Investigation: health and well-being

Stage of process	Text	Duration	Numbers involved
finding co-investigators	invitation to ALP members	2 weeks	
co-investigation	questionnaire, interviewing skills, interviewing relatives & neighbours, weekly meetings	8 weeks	9
decoding	targeted on groups of unemployed, women and pensioners	5 weeks	35
learning/action programmes	Living Memory Project, Programme for Unemployment/ Loose End Activity Centre, Women and Well-being	2 years / 16 weeks / 30 weeks	30 / 31 / 44

Health and Well-being has been selected for inclusion because it is ALP's second major investigation, showing significant adaptations of the process in the light of lessons learned from the first. It is more focalized: on health, on unemployed people, women, and elderly people. It marks the emergence of the theme of good communication between people as a vital component of well-being, and it contains attempts to integrate learning and action within each programme.

Co-investigation

A cross-section of ALP members were invited to become co-investigators. A questionnaire was devised to give a common structure to interviews and make it easier to collate and analyse the data. Questions included:

Do you enjoy your work?

How does work/unemployment affect your health and the health of others in your family?

Have you any interests or hobbies?

Do you feel financially secure?

What part do friends and relations play in your life?

When you're feeling bad do you have someone you can talk to?

How often do you visit the doctor?

What sort of things do you do which are good or bad for your health?

What would you like to do to improve your health or your sense of well-being?

In the first session co-investigators practised the skills of interviewing on each other. The next few weeks were spent interviewing relations, friends and neighbours, and observing moments of life at the doctor's surgery, the baby clinic, a hospital ward, the DHSS office, the job centre, local shops and cafes, a pensioners' association meeting, and the day centre for the elderly. Co-investigators were asked to take responsibility for recording and analysing their interviews and observations. While co-investigators were sharing their findings, common threads were noticed in interviews with people whose circumstances were similar. It was decided to group these interviews under the following headings: housewives, single workers, married workers, unemployed people, and pensioners.

Most interviewees were physically well and had little contact with the health service. In any case, they saw going to the doctor as a last resort. Good communication with others – partners, relatives, friends, bosses, officials – was very important. Housewives felt their daytime contact with others, outside the nursery school, at the shops, or on the stair, was too superficial. Single people put a lot of energy into their social life outside work. The unemployed were often cut off from their friends through lack of cash. Married couples could not always rely on one another for real communication. One couple in their forties, both working, with teenage children, realized during the interview that the husband's grumpiness at home was related to boredom at work. The wife had been too busy and fulfilled in her own job to realize it.

Interviewees were well informed about the causes of ill-health but did not always adopt a healthy lifestyle. For instance, an overweight woman, who would like to have gone on a particular diet, couldn't afford the cost of the food involved. A tight budget was the cause of worry for many young families and unemployed people, and prevented them from doing things like socializing or taking part in sports, which could have contributed to their sense of well-being.

Building codifications and decoding

Members of the Photo Workshop helped to build codifications appropriate to the life situations of each group. Training sessions were arranged for co-investigators who volunteered to act as co-ordinators or observer/recorders in the decoding discussions. Decoding lasted five weeks and took place not only in the ALP Shop but also in a local church hall with a mother and toddler group, and in a day centre with elderly people.

The decoding sessions with elderly people took the form of in-depth interviews with two or three people at a time. The focus was on their memories of living and working in Gorgie Dalry in the 1930s and 1940s. This lead to the creation of the Living Memory Project in collaboration with St Bride's Community Centre.

Unemployed

The unemployed group discussed photographs depicting moments in an unemployed man's day: Questions included:

What can you tell about this man from the pictures?
How does he feel about people at the job centre, at the DHSS?
How do they feel about him?
How does his income affect what he buys at the supermarket?
How does unemployment affect relationships in the family?
Do you have a hobby?
How does the media portray people on the dole?
What do you feel about someone who works on the side?

A major contradiction emerged between feelings of being excluded, no longer needed or useful, and feelings of release from boring jobs, with time to do other things. Shortage of cash and dependence on the bureaucracy was a problem. So was the need to replace the discipline imposed by work with self-discipline. The block was identified as lack of motivation, and the task for learning/action programmes was to find ways of overcoming inertia.

14. Unemployment – at home

Loose End Activity Centre

Out of these discussions arose a decision by the decoding group to set up the Loose End Activity Centre in Gorgie Memorial Hall, open to unemployed people and others available during the day. It offered a Programme for Unemployment which aimed to help people gain a better understanding of what was happening to them, how unemployment was affecting their relationships with others, and how they might respond in a positive way. The programme also included running a food co-operative and an information centre, music-making, and putting on fund-raising dances to pay for out-of-door recreational activities.

Women

Codifications designed for decoding by groups of mothers with young children included photographs of two women in close conversation, scenes from the baby clinic, a mother feeding her baby, and sketches of a woman doing housework. Questions included:

> How does being a mother affect your sense of well-being?
> How much contact do you have with other adults during the day?
> Do you have a close friend?
> What do mothers feel when they're at the baby clinic?
> Is it easy to discuss things with the health visitor and the doctor?
> How does housework compare with the work you did before you got married?

Statements made in response included:

> I feel the family needs me. I can't afford to be ill. But I know if I neglect myself the whole family suffers.

> A good natter's very important. It releases tension. You need a friend you can say anything to.

> You get nervous at the baby clinic. You feel you're being judged.

And referring to a sympathetic clinic doctor:

> She's a bit scatty, you feel on equal terms.

> She gives you information that's easy to digest.

> She takes time to talk.

Themes and contradictions emerging included: the sense of being part of a family, versus a loss of individual identity; a feeling of doing a worthwhile job as a mother, versus a lack of recognition and an excess of responsibility. The main block was feelings of guilt at taking time for yourself, and the task was to take the time, and find ways of building up your health mentally and physically.

Women and Well-being

It was decided that the learning programmes would incorporate action for health. Two groups were planned, one during the day for mothers of young children, with a creche, and one in the evening for a mixed group of women. Responsibility for running them would be shared between the ALP workers and trained ALP volunteers, and participants would be asked to sign on for the whole programme. In this way was introduced for the first time the idea of an explicit contract between individuals and the project. In the daytime group, mothers often found it difficult at first to leave their children in the creche, and turn their attention to the session. Some of the ways the group got over this included asking members to hand in thumbnail sketches of their children, inviting creche workers into the group to make regular progress reports, and having calm-down exercises at the start of each session.

The plan was to start by identifying blocks and then move on to ways of tackling them. Participants looked at their roots, at themselves as children growing up in a particular place, at a particular time, within a particular family. Guided fantasy was used to help participants feel their way back into those early situations, and afterwards they wrote about people who had been important to them in childhood.

Then members looked at the 'messages' they had received from their parents and others, the values that were being transmitted and the extent to which they were still influential. These sessions helped people get some perspective on the past. They also served to highlight the very different backgrounds and experiences of members.

Now it was the turn of the present. Members were invited to assess their current state of well-being using a scale to help them pick out areas of satisfaction and frustration in their lives. This was an individual exercise carried out at home, to help members focus on their own blocks to well-being. They were asked to choose one and write about it. They included: the time and energy needed for children; loss of the status which employment gives; the lack of satisfying conversation with other adults; financial dependence on husbands; general loss of confidence and fear of criticism; weight problems possibly linked to stress; chronic lack of sleep; tension caused by carrying their husbands' often work-related anxiety; and serious illness in the family causing relationship problems.

Moving into a more active mode, resource people were invited in to run a series of workshops on self-image, food and body awareness. These were funny, informative and energizing but not always tuned to action on the blocks identified by the group. This highlighed once again the importance of briefing resource people, so that their knowledge dovetailed well with the group's requirements.

By the end of term, all the groups had succeeded in addressing one of the key blocks to well-being: the lack of opportunities for satisfying communication with other adults. The skills of dialogue had become part of the course content. Members had been asked to

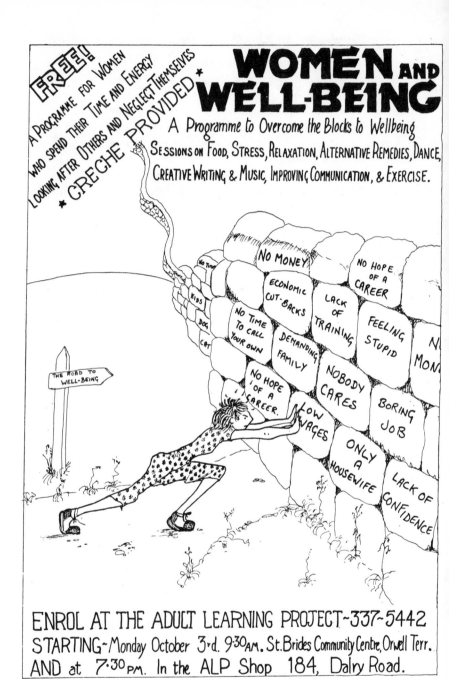

15. Women and Well-being leaflet

practise listening in small groups and reporting back in the larger group. They had also been asked to prepare for sessions and reflect on them afterwards, causing dialogue to spill over into the streets, with people talking to each other and members of their family between sessions.

The second term, after the break, picked up on a theme which had emerged strongly concerning the relationship between mothers and daughters. Members were asked to prepare a collage in words and symbols of four generations in their families: grandmother, mother, self, and daughter or son. A pattern emerged in the group: images of older generations were strongly positive or negative, images of the self were dull and low-key, and images of children were positive and lively. Evidently most of the hope was still invested in the future and in their children. The women themselves were almost invisible, waiting in the wings.

Other exercises were used. Members described in detail how a recent meeting with their mothers had gone, and how they would like to replay it. Working in small groups they found out more about how others in the group saw them. They shared with the group a collage done at home on aspects of their personalities which did not find expression in their role as mothers. They drew their life-line, marking off significant dates and events, and choosing one turning point to write about. These included breaking off an engagement, adopting a baby, moving from one country to another, affording a washing-machine, getting a part-time job, surviving a serious illness, and coping with death in the family. One reason for this exercise was to encourage individuals to see the possibility of creating another turning-point by choosing to tackle blocks in the present.

As a spur and support to action the term was rounded off with sessions on yoga, relaxation exercises, and an introduction to alternative medicine. Members were asked to keep a diary over Easter, noting things which contributed to a sense of well-being.

In the third term the focus was on the present, on their roles as parents responsible for children's health. Children had been deliberately side-lined until now, but they were never far away! Resource people were invited in to advise members about dealing with children's minor ailments themselves, and to give new ideas for playing with children.

By the end of the programme, the group wanted to re-draw the publicity leaflet, changing the wall made of blocks of stone into a

16. Women in conversation in the street

gate which once successfully passed through, would lead to more maturity and strength.

Review

One woman summed things up in writing for the review session at the end:

> I dug out the original handout I'd picked up telling me about the ALP Women and Well-being group. What had attracted me to it? I like the way it made me feel important, worth getting to know and worth helping to develop. The idea of commitment seemed important to me too. A stable group meeting regularly over a longish period of time could actually achieve something. It seemed worth finding out about. In addition, so many words in the handout rang bells for me: 'identity' was there, and 'guilty', and 'communication' . . .
>
> Throughout the sessions I've been amazed at how much we all

17. At the baby clinic – waiting

have in common, and how much mutual support can be made available, as opposed to the kind of isolation you can feel when no such group is around. The kind of good, honest communication that goes on in the group is something that I feel I need more of now that I've experienced it. Too often communication can be just at a shallow, sociable level and can seem very meaningless. It's one of the few groups I've attended where I feel my opinions are worth airing, and where I feel my absence would really be noticed. As a result of being a group member I've reached the conclusion that a means of increasing my well-being would be to feel myself an important part of the organizational side of some group. I need to give to something, rather than just continue to attend groups as a member. I think I'm looking for some sort of role like I had at work.

Two of the women and well-being groups continued to meet on a self-supporting basis for a further period. A third group met socially in each other's homes.

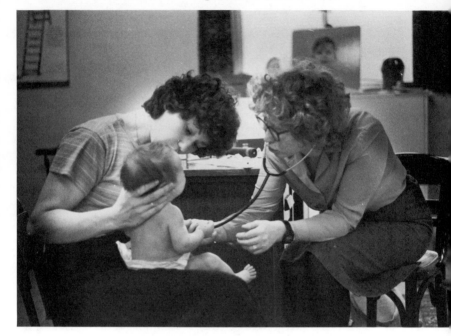

18. At the baby clinic – consultation with a doctor

Issues arising from Health and Well-being

- There was a general fear on the part of participants of being asked to help co-ordinate the group.
- The unemployed group was divided into two factions, one wanting to find work, the other seeing the positive side of being released from boring work and free to do other things. Each faction disapproved of the other.
- The move by some members of the unemployed decoding group to go straight into action by setting up the Loose End Activity Centre, an ambitious project requiring a lot of worker support, may have been premature and was not well researched in advance.
- The practice of making a contract with members of learning programmes was introduced for the first time during this investigation. It is unusual in community education settings to make such demands of participants.
- The use of resource people to promote action for health created a problem. These sessions had to be planned and the resource

people booked in advance, which meant that their contributions did not arise in response to the specific blocks identified by participants.

• A criticism made of the Women and Well-being programme was that it attempted to cover too much ground in each session and in the programme as a whole.

3. Investigation: parents and authority

Stage of process	Text	Duration	Numbers involved
finding co-investigators	members of women and well-being groups and their neighbours	2 weeks	
co-investigation	sharing experiences of authority, family and upbringing, interviewing friends, relatives, weekly meetings	6 weeks	21
decoding	same people, themes of risk and security, negotiation and authoritarianism in parenting	2 weeks	21
learning programme	Parents, Children and Authority – how Britain compares with other countries	10 weeks	26

Parents and Authority has been chosen for inclusion as a case study because it demonstrates significant developments in the ALP process. The members of a Women and Well-being learning group agreed to become co-investigators, and doubled their numbers by recruiting from among their friends and neighbours. A core of people continued to be involved from the start of co-investigation right through to the action stage. Participants were asked to take more responsibility for every aspect of the process, which was dramatically speeded up.

Co-investigation and decoding were more closely linked and treated as two phases of one stage of the process, involving the same group of people. They became, in effect, the first stage of the learning programme.

During the learning programme itself, fewer resource people were

used, more intensively, and there was more careful dovetailing of the
new knowledge presented with the questions raised by participants.
Ample time was built in for members to dialogue with each other
and with the resource people over a series of meetings.

Choosing the theme

The ALP workers had sometimes found themselves talking at cross-
purposes with people who saw authority only as the possession of
those with power over others. The notion of personal authority not
deriving from an official position but as an integral part of the
identity of individuals, was difficult to grasp. But more and more
ALP members were being encouraged to use their own authority in
the various roles they took on within the project. The workers also
knew that parents were concerned about how to discipline their
children at a time when attitudes to authority in society were
changing.

Co-investigation

The idea was that co-investigators would begin by sharing their
experiences of authority with each other, and use what they were
finding out in the group as a springboard for their interviews with
others. They would go on to build their own codifications of the
themes they were identifying, and learn how to decode them in the
group. Finally, selecting the most generative theme, they would
decide on a learning programme and get as close as possible to
building the curriculum themselves.

Twenty-one parents including two fathers arrived for the first of
six sessions. The ALP workers outlined the task and the methods to
be used, and divided the group in two. They began with brief
discussions of the meaning of authority, starting with the dictionary
definition and encouraging participants to make the distinction
between titular and personal authority.

The parents said they felt uninvolved in the exercise of authority in
the titular sense, and sometimes felt treated like children by the
authorities. Personal authority was described as a quality which
some people just have. They have presence, they have knowledge
and skills, and they are worth listening to. They are freely given
respect.

The second session was about our experiences of authority in childhood. Participants brought family pictures showing them in the company of parents, grandparents, brothers and sisters. They had been asked to think about the following questions:

Who had authority over you as a child?
What did their authority derive from?
How did you react to it?
How much scope did you have to develop your own authority as a child?

In the discussions, some common threads could be identified. It seemed that fathers and mothers had exercised quite different kinds of authority, the one symbolic, the other real. Fathers were described as strong, silent and absent most of the time. They were impractical and needed looking after. Mothers were responsible for day-to-day discipline, and tended to rule their children's lives. But somehow, because they were more accessible, their authority was less absolute. The hand of parents was strengthened if it was backed up by external authority; father's job, the church, a political party or even the values of a particular class to which the parents aspired.

At the third session, co-investigators reported on interviews they had done with friends and relatives. The questions had been modified to encourage interviewees to speak concretely about their experiences. They now read:

Who were the key authority figures in your childhood?
Can you remember any incidents which show how you reacted to them?
How much scope did you have, inside or outside the family, to express yourself as an individual?
What were people's attitudes to authority when you were growing up?

One co-investigator reported the response of a woman whose childhood authority figures were the nuns at her school. She described an incident where she took money from the gas meter to go swimming, got as far as the bus-stop and went home and put it back. God was the authority!

Another woman had grown up in a village in the south of England before the war, where authority was all-embracing:

The village bobby was a father figure, feared, respected and trusted. He was consulted about trivial things. There was a closeness between the police, the school and the home. The burden of authority was taken off parents' shoulders by these key authority figures. There was *no* questioning of authority. All adults, even bus conductors, had more respect than children. People generally approved of authority and disapproved of anyone who went against it. There was an overall feeling of being desperate to remain secure.

Most interviewees had found ways of asserting themselves:

I was the best fighter in the class.

I got praise for being good at drawing.

I was good at building dams.

I could go a two-wheeler when everyone else could only go a three-wheeler.

I was in a drama class at school and showed them all how to dance.

Another way of asserting your difference was by being bad – being a rebel, lying to avoid trouble, and deflating authority figures by laughing at them or running rings round them.

But the consensus emerging from the interviews seemed to be that questioning authority, even in your head, had been a painful process. As children, those interviewed had been aware of the risk of disapproval or the withdrawal of love.

In the fourth session co-investigators discussed their role as parents. Questions they had been asked to think about were:

Can you describe an incident that illustrates the authority relationship between you and your child?

What do you do to encourage your child's independence?

What are the changes in attitudes to authority since you were a child?

How does society help or hinder you as a parent in the 1980s?

They worked first in pairs to warm themselves up, then continued the dialogue in the large group. An incident described by one member had echoes for the others, and she was asked to write it up.

I was watering the window-box the other day. The window has to be wide open. My son Alan was pottering around but as soon as the watering started he wanted to join in and held up a milk bottle to be filled with water so that he could help. I explained that it was too dangerous for him to water the window-box because he might fall out of the window but that he could help me to water the other plants later. He then threw the milk bottle as hard as he could onto the kitchen floor. I was angry with him and told him how dangerous broken glass was. I said he would have to go and fetch the dustpan and brush. He did so with great enthusiasm – he loves sweeping-up – but he became very angry again because I refused to allow him to help. He *was* allowed to tell me where there were bits of broken glass.

Sometimes I find it difficult to pursue a hard line I've started on. I felt mean not allowing him to do any sweeping-up when he was so enthusiastic about collecting the dustpan and brush. But it was dangerous and I felt anyway he shouldn't enjoy the fruits of his misbehaviour. The problem is you want your child to be happy *and* well-behaved. And you want a quiet life for yourself.

At the fifth session, the co-investigators reported back on more interviews, this time about people's experience of being parents.

Their findings can be summed up as follows: parents encouraged their children's authority by allowing them more privacy, admitting their own mistakes, and expecting their child to be responsible for their own behaviour, within a framework of rules. In general they were trying to operate regimes which were less repressive than those of their own parents, to be more approachable, more open and more honest. But society itself had become more threatening, and the children were less free to wander and play out of sight than they had been.

Summary of themes emerging

The task of identifying the emerging themes was approached by sifting through the records of sessions, selecting out key statements, grouping them, and naming the themes and contradictions implicit in them, as follows:

- In the past, when there was more general agreement about how to bring up children, some children used to find scope for self-expression by subverting the rules, but others were ground down by them.
- In today's small family, there is more negotiation between parents and children, but the scope for parental repression and authoritarianism remains.

19. Children learning to sew

- Discipline and fear of danger keep children safe – but children need to be allowed to take risks in order to become independent.
- Children are tolerated less in Britain than in other countries. The underlying feeling is that kids equals chaos. They must be controlled, or else they will destroy both us and themselves.

These emergent themes were further summarized as *negotiation versus authoritarianism*, and *risk versus security*.

Building codifications

Co-investigators who were interested in helping to build codifications were invited to an extra session. Participants found it easy to suggest situations embodying the themes, but they were limited to what a camera could capture. It would have been almost impossible, for example, to get a photo of the child smashing the milk bottle! The pictures it was decided to take were: a mother at the sewing machine with children cutting out nearby; a small girl in the backgreen holding an adult-sized fork; the same girl behind her garden gate

20. Boys jumping off the weir at Cramond

watching other children play in the street; a mother and child on a pre-enrolment visit to school. Another unplanned photograph was taken because one of the group members happened to be in the right place at the right time to capture an incident embodying the theme of risk and security: a shot of boys jumping off the weir at Cramond.

Decoding

The decoding process was shortened to two sessions, for which the groups were brought together. The first meeting was intended to be a teach-in on decoding rather than a full decoding session. All the photographs were presented briefly except one. Participants responded spontaneously, even before any questions were asked. Here are some of their comments on the picture of the boys jumping off the weir at Cramond:

- I can't bear to think about it. They're aiming for a deep hole, but the water around it's very shallow.

- They're thrilled because they can do it.
- They're feeling brave coping with danger. But you worry in case some of the boys are leading the others on.
- Looking at it makes me feel I wish I wasn't so frightened about things.

For the second session the two groups were kept together. This was a properly structured decoding discussion, with one ALP worker leading and the other recording. They chose the picture of the little girl behind the garden gate, watching other children playing in the street. The theme encoded was risk and security. A verbatim record of the early part of the session is presented here, to give the reader a flavour of the experience of decoding.

What's happening in the picture?

- Children playing on bikes, some of them on the road.
- One child's looking through a fence.
- That's Katy! The gate's shut.
- There's no traffic, the street's a dead-end.
- There're no adults in sight. It's all kids. There's a minibus parked on the other side of the road.
- It's a sunny day. That child's going very fast on her bike.
- Later on there'll be cars parked on both sides of the road, even though it's against the law.
- The child on the pavement – the smallest one away at the end of the terrace – he looks very young, too young to be out.
- That's my son!

Tell me about the rest of the terraces, the situation round about.

- There's a road at the end of the street. There're cars parked in the square in the middle of the terraces.
- All the houses have gardens.
- The main road's not far away – it's a death trap.
- The wee ones know they're not allowed to go beyond the square.
- People look out for other people's children. The terraces has that feel. The houses are all very close together.
- Young families want to live there because it's safe compared to other areas. You're prepared to put up with living so close together.

21. Children playing in the street

As well as making you feel safe, does living close together have its drawbacks?

- I like closeness. It goes along with safety. In the country you've got more space and privacy, but you don't feel so safe. It's a close community. Children walking in pyjamas will be brought back. People know you.
- But you have to toe the line. There's a neighbour watches every move I make. You're only supposed to put your washing out at certain times of the day. If it rains and my washing's out she phones me up.
- Yes, I was having a conversation with a friend about marriage guidance. People in the next garden could hear. I felt it was too near the bone.
- There's a price to be paid for safety. You have to conform to normal behaviour, for example getting up early and not arguing too loudly with your husband.

OK lets's look again at the picture. What are the problems for kids playing in the terraces?

- Well, sometimes if a car wants to reverse into the terrace, you need to organize the kids off the road first. You just hope that people driving in know it's an area where children play.
- Some of us tried to get play-street signs put up, but the police say fathers drive fast so what good would a sign do? Cars are the problem, not kids.
- After school for a while the streets belong to the kids. Then people come home from work and there's double-parking, especially in Hazelbank. Hazelbank's not as safe as some of the other terraces. But the children look out for one another.

They seem unconcerned in the photo: they're not playing together or aware of each other.

- But there's an electric current goes up the street when a car comes. The kids are told not to go beyond the end of the street. Suzanne's allowed to play at the other end of the terrace over Shaftsbury Park. But she has to be brought back. She'd wet herself rather than cross alone. She knows she wouldn't be allowed out to play if she did.
- Katy's watching the other children play from behind her garden wall.
- I know. She's desperate to get out.

Why take the risk? Why not just keep children indoors where they're safe?

- Children need to learn about traffic. They need to play together.
- They'd climb over the gate. They'd get out somehow.
- Parents take a balanced risk.
- If you keep them in, you have to cope with their fury.

What are the children getting out of the situation?

- You want them to mix and be independent of you.
- There's no space in back gardens for bikes.
- Kids are learning how to socialize, how to live with other people, including older people. Not to go on the motor-bike at the corner.

- But letting children out to play means more work for the parents. You're never away from the window.
- There's pressure on parents, because other kids are allowed out to play at a young age.

Other themes emerging in the later part of this decoding session were named as *security and conformity; fear of freedom*; and *the family against society*.

Building the curriculum

The co-investigators were asked to read the records of their meetings so far, and come up with questions which they would like to pursue further as part of a learning programme. One woman contributed her comments in writing. She dismissed the agonizing that had been going on about disciplining children:

> True authority is not about the practical details of child-rearing. It's about the parents having a real sense of identity. If they know who they are and what they're doing in life, that will communicate itself immediately to their children. We have been saying that we can develop personal authority only by participating in the real world, accepting responsibility, and taking risks. But for me the problem is that our society operates a very sharp divide between the world of children and the world of adults. Children are barely tolerated on social occasions, and almost never in the workplace. They're expected to behave, obey, and conform, without being given the opportunity to mature. The majority of children reach parenthood without the faintest idea of what it's all about. Most girls of sixteen or seventeen, given the experience of looking after children and housekeeping, would make good mothers, but not if they've spent their lives at a school desk, failing exams. We don't allow our children to grow up, and this has sad consequences for our teenagers.

The questions she posed for further learning were: How do we break down the barrier that exists between children and adults in our society? Do other countries integrate their children more successfully? Do we have to re-think our whole approach to education?

The idea for a cross-cultural programme emerged. The group wanted to look at ways other countries bring up their children with a view to learning from them. They would invite parents from other cultures to join in.

Learning programme

The programme was called Parents, Children and Authority – how Britain compares with other countries. The blurb on the publicity leaflet summarized the theme:

> Parents in every country want to bring up their children well. What this means in practice will be different in different countries and at different times. But we have a lot in common. We want to keep our children safe and give them a sense of security. At the same time we want them to grow up into mature adults – responsible, self-disciplined and creative. To do that they have to be allowed to take risks. In the next ten weeks we will be exploring the conflicts which all parents share and identifying the ways different cultures have of tackling them.

The outline programme ran like this:

Session 1. Introductions to each other and to the creche.
2. Growing up in our parents home.
3. The influence of our culture. Focus on adolescence.
4. Presentation by a Scottish psychologist.
5. Presentation by a Kenyan psychologist.
6. Comparing our experience with what the psychologists said.
7. Dialogue with both psychologists present.
8. Bringing up children in Scotland today: identifying problems.
9. Two members (from different countries) each present a parenting problem.
10. Review of the programme and proposals for action.
11. Social in the creche, with food from different countries.

In the session about being brought up in our parents' home, the questions asked were:

What were the rules in *your* home, and what were the values implied by them?
Which parent had most authority/responsibility in your family?

What was your relationship to brothers and sisters?
Which adult in your family has had most influence over you?

The Pakistani women said that girls in their country were expected to speak quietly, and be quiet at table. From the age of 10, they had to cover their heads and not speak to boys. The Koran guided every aspect of life in their culture. Reading the Koran and confessing your sins to a mullah brought forgiveness, blessing and the approval of relatives. As Salma said, obedience to religion 'makes God *and* mother happy.'

Children growing up in rural areas were governed by fewer rules relating to their safety. Anne from Finland recalled running along the seashore and wandering home through the woods after dark. Constantia described her son on holiday back in Cyprus as being like a wild animal let out of a cage. There was general agreement that parents today had enjoyed greater physical freedom than their children.

Another key point to emerge was that girls experienced authority very differently from boys, especially in cultures where the division of roles between the sexes was strictest.

In the session on participants' experience of adolescence, the question was: 'How easy was it for you to challenge the authority of your parents?' Some members challenged the assumption that it was necessary to rebel.

In Pakistan a high value was placed on getting on with everyone. Others were disposed to see rebellion as a kind of distortion, the result of an individualistic and competitive culture. Only a few admitted to having been rebellious. Out of this discussion, the following questions were distilled and sent to the visiting resource people, to guide their contributions.

How much autonomy should adolescents have?
Is it necessary to rebel in adolescence?
What are the risks involved in rebellion?
How are boys and girls affected in their development by a strict division between the sexes?
How important is strong religious faith in children's development?
How are children affected by the social class aspirations of their parents?
How do the restrictions caused by living in the city affect children?

The next session was a presentation by a Scottish psychologist, Janet Hassan, on the basic conditions for the healthy development of children, and how these were affected by culture. She was asked to make her contribution in the light of participants' questions, and challenge them in their role as parents. Extracts from Janet's presentation are presented here to give the reader a sense of the part played by new knowledge in a learning programme. An attempt is made to portray the experience of the session, as intimate and provocative, rather than to give a bland summary of content and concepts.

I can define myself by my nationality, social class, religion, or the particular family to which I belong, but there is the additional question – *who am I?* There is no family or group of any kind where members are all the same. We hold family rituals to re-establish membership. But we are different from one another. As individuals we may resent being seen just as a member of some group. For example, I am an old-aged pensioner but I am more than that. I get angry when people expect me to behave in certain ways befitting an old lady.

We grow from the cradle to the grave. It's useful to think of growing in the form of a spiral rather than steps and stairs with each stage of development finished before the next one begins. Growth in the form of a spiral is a continuous process – there are times when you feel like a baby or an adolescent, at any age. We are all that we have experienced. The experience is there in the spiral. It is possible to reach back into it to help us with parenting our own children. For example in dealing with an adolescent, recognizing at the same time that he lives in a different world.

Inside any adult, there are all sorts of levels of experience. The question is: which one do I use when responding to the toddler having a tantrum, or the adolescent who is asserting her right to have a good time despite the risks. Parents' feelings, related to their past experience, can get in the way of good discipline, for example, the mother who envies her adolescent daughter the good time she is having. Do I ask myself: 'Why am I responding in this way', or do I fall back on what my mother would have said or what others in the culture say, or what books say. The children are *your* children.

As individual human beings we have a choice – to grow up or

not. Living is about growing. Some people are happy to remain as children all their lives. They have narrow spirals with limited experience and little thinking about experience. Mummy (or some other authority) will tell us what to do. It is the duty of all religions to tell us to grow up. Politicians sometimes seem to be trying to prevent people growing up.

In different cultures there are different traditions of child-rearing. But the basic needs of children for healthy growth and development are the same. All children need:

Attachment

Children need to know who they are attached to, which family, which group. Children who know to whom they belong have a basic optimism in life. Things that may affect attachment and the identity of the child include: Are you valued as a boy, as a girl? Are you wanted by your parents, or only by your grandparents? Does your family stay put or move from one culture to another, for example, from a culture which emphasizes communal identity, to one which emphasizes individual identity? Is attachment to one person in the first year of life (though not necessarily the mother – fathers who have been properly mothered have a bit of their mother inside them, and can mother their children)?

Giving and receiving affection

The child in the family needs to grow out of narcissism to consider other people. The child in the high chair is brought to the family table, and has to wait his or her turn for attention. Bringing children up to make choices involves discipline. People make choices within limits. Parents need to use authority. Children need to learn to belong to the group.

Stimulation

Children need it. Adults too. We respond to stimulation, for example, in the physical environment. What is our environment in the home and surrounding district saying to us? Is it saying we are worthwhile or worthless? Women are aware more than men that visitors will be stimulated and respond to the environment they have created in the home. Relationships in the family are another kind of stimulus. What is the message to the child of mother and father fighting?

Identity
Family identity, sexual identity, cultural identity, how others define us. Family identity: some children are told (not necessarily in so many words) you will be like your father, mother, etc. They may passively accept their given identity, or get angry and struggle to assert their difference. The family identity may be at odds with the identity of other families round about. It may be difficult for the family to hold its own against the neighbourhood. Parents have to believe that they can influence what families are about and what neighbours are about. We are members one of another, but we are also individuals who can influence the way others behave. This is true of other aspects of our identity which we inherit through the culture we are born into. To make what we are given ours, that is, part of our personal identity, we need to challenge it and make choices about what suits us.

Groups
The identity of the individual is tested in his or her membership of groups. Getting on in groups is *not* about conforming, because that may mean you lose your identity. It's about co-operating out of your own authority and identity.

Responsibility
Only if earlier parts of the process have been successfully negotiated (attachment, giving and receiving affection, stimulation, identity, and membership of groups) will the individual be capable of responsibility.

Janet summed up:

Being alive is being in conflict.

The next session was a presentation by another psychologist, this time from Kenya. Sarah Sieley was able to relate her knowledge of psychological processes to a very personal account of her journey across the boundaries of several cultures. She agreed that children's needs for security, recognition, group membership, and responsibility were universal. But different societies meet these basic needs in very different ways.

Her own story began in a village of 200 people in Kenya.

From the age of five, children were given lots of responsibility for important survival tasks, for example stopping cows from eating maize, collecting firewood, and preventing a younger child from falling into the open fire. Children gained recognition for the successful completion of tasks. Punishment for failing was harsh and consistent. It was a very authoritarian regime.

At the American mission school, she learned to compete. That was the beginning of her individuality, and represented a clash with values at home where the emphasis was on conformity and obedience. Later, she went away to secondary school and her life became very different from those with whom she had played as a child.

Between the ages of 12–14 the village children underwent the secret rites which marked the passage from childhood into adulthood. Boys and girls were circumcised and were taught by the Elders of the village. Adolescence as a phase was not recognized. Girls were given away in return for a dowry, while boys married and lived in the family unit.

Through education Sarah gained another identity which was socially acceptable in the village since educated members of the family could be expected to help others. She studied in Nairobi and in the United States, married an Englishman, and came to live in Edinburgh. She learned that, in Britain, a child of nine was considered too young to babysit. She found relationships at work very formal. Invitations to dinner were given a fortnight in advance. You couldn't just drop in at someone's house. She had no natural networks of friends and relations, and concluded that you had to go out and get a network. People needed to interact with others in order to feel themselves.

She met prejudice in Edinburgh, and had to defend her personal identity against the stereotype that black women were either nurses or students. Society in Edinburgh was more complex than in a rural village in Kenya. The child here met lots of strangers in the street, often experiencing herself and others as individuals rather than as members of a particular group. She wondered if that was why individuality was rewarded in Britain. Was it linked to survival, just as conformity and obedience was linked to survival in the Kenyan village?

Immigrants to Britain felt threatened. The individualistic majority culture was trying to swallow them up. So the family group became even more important for identity than it would have been, say, in Pakistan. Immigrants could suffer from cultural schizophrenia.

In the discussion which followed, a group member challenged

Sarah's assertion that Britain was an individualistic society. He argued that there was conformity to smaller sub-groups. Another member said that she was trying to bring up her children her own way, but was aware that often parents looked to their neighbours for an example and did as the street culture dictated.

Members discussed the emphasis Janet had placed on the infant's need for attachment to one person in the first year of life, and the contrast with the Kenyan village where childcare was shared by a number of adults. The group agreed that what was important was consistent, caring handling, a dependable routine, even if child-care was shared.

Immigrant parents highlighted the loss experienced by their children, in only rarely seeing their relatives. Others who had moved within Britain agreed: children needed to belong to grandparents, too. The importance of keeping in touch with the culture of origin as far as possible was stressed, but there was also a need to adapt to the local culture. This widened out into an exploration of clashes of cultures experienced by both parents and children. Some anxiety was expressed about the danger of children becoming confused. Sarah agreed in response that children could take in all sorts of differences. They needed a very strong background to criss-cross between the different cultures and sub-cultures in Britain, and make good choices.

The sixth session was a dialogue in small groups, the purpose of which was to help participants integrate the new knowledge contained in the presentations, and to select the questions for the psychologists' return visit the following week.

The group felt that the two presentations had given a lift to the whole programme. They had reacted strongly to Janet's presentation. She had emphasized individual responsibility, the need to exercise authority, and the value of being different. She had used words like challenge, and conflict. That seemed to spoil the good feeling they had got out of listening to people from societies which knew the meaning of community, and emphasized the value of co-operation over competition. The questions they wanted to feed back to the resource people included:

How does giving and receiving affection link to discipline?
How can we use our authority as parents, but avoid being authoritarian?

Can children learn to co-operate and conform, and at the same time maintain their individual identity?

Is competition necessary for the development of a strong identity?

Is the emphasis on individuality in Britain bad for us?

How important is respect for elders?

In the dialogue between the group and the psychologists, most of the questions were directed at Janet.

You seem to be saying we have to challenge everything we get from our parents?

JANET: Being a copy of your parents and your culture of origin unquestioningly is bad. But if you examine your culture and decide to take aspects on board, that's fine.

I must admit I was quite angry at you saying we had to challenge everything and grow up. It's not as easy as all that.

If you challenge, you risk losing the love of those close to you.

Is it an either/or situation, either you grow up or you remain a child?

JANET: Part of being an adult is to acknowledge your own needs. This includes your need to be a child sometimes. But it is important to monitor your behaviour, and be conscious of when you are satisfying needs in yourself. And challenge isn't the same as rejection. If you challenge a situation, and change it, you're more likely to be committed to it.

I don't want to be always challenging things and changing them. I feel too responsible as it is. If you're a parent, you're never allowed to be irresponsible.

Other countries seem to offer more support to parents.

JANET: There's a myth that somewhere there is a contented cul-true. Every culture has its difficulties. One of our difficulties is that we have an excess of individualism and competition.

The trick is to co-operate with others out of our own authority and individuality. This is something we all have to struggle with, whatever our cultural background. Societies, like individuals, can't stay the same. They have to grow.

Back home

In sessions eight and nine it was back to small groups. The workers asked:

> What problems do *you* have bringing up your children in Edinburgh?

There was a lot of agreement about the kinds of problems facing parents, whether of the host or immigrant community. The latter experienced the same problems, but in a more exaggerated form. For example, the problem of being stuck with your kids twenty-four hours a day – and them being stuck with you; the need for a support system to replace the support once offered by the extended family, but not one which is institutionalized; the problem for immigrants of passing on the tradition, without allowing the old culture to become frozen, integrating good things from the adopted culture; and the fear of outside influences undermining the family's values.

In the last session, before the celebration in the creche, the groups came together to review the programme and decide on a possible course of action to tackle the problems identified.

The co-ordinator reminded the group of the origin of the cross-cultural initiative: a desire on the part of British parents to learn from other cultures. What they had found was: extended families offering their members support; children given responsibility at an earlier age; family values echoed in the community; shared religious faith; a tradition of story-telling; respect for elders; less class-consciousness; fewer dangers and more freedom for children. But the price to pay was often a more authoritarian society.

The resource people had helped by suggesting that it was possible to overcome the dichotomy between excessive individualism and group conformity, by co-operating out of one's authority and identity.

The group decided that there were two categories of problems: those that concerned internal relationships within the family, and those involving the relationship of the family with the rest of the community.

Action

The course of action proposed was to create a Parents' Centre which would be open to all parents in the area and especially parents from other cultures. It would be run by its own members, with the support of ALP staff. There would be learning programmes, and scope for individual parents to talk about problems. And there would be a well-run creche.

Issues arising from Parents and Authority

- The workers were almost too successful in bringing together people who shared the same life circumstances. They were all parents of young children, mostly from the same part of Gorgie Dalry, who shared many of the same values. This made it difficult to bring out some of the contradictions. At the same time, it made for a very focalized investigation, and made it easier for participants to co-operate, and set up social support systems.

- One and a half hours was the maximum time that could be allowed for sessions involving parents of small children who are constrained by having to drop children off at school and pick them up again. Such a short time sometimes made it harder to get into sustained analysis.

- Ambitions for the multi-cultural aspect of the project were only partly realized. The participants from other countries were in-comers into an already established group. They were also a minority. The intention was that they would become full members, but in practice the language problem was more inhibiting than had been anticipated. Much more time would have been required to build up good communications with the immigrant communities for the multi-cultural potential of the project to be fully realized.

- When the presentation of new knowledge is good and pro-vocative, a lot of heat is generated. The group – or at least some members of it – can get down to exploring fundamental values, which can link people across the boundaries of different cultures. Sufficient time needs to be allowed for further explo-ration and articulation of values, and this can cause problems in a programme which is structured in advance.

Note of acknowledgement

The authors acknowledge the contributions of Janet Hassan and Sarah Sieley to this chapter. Sarah's contribution is printed without her express permission, since we have been unable to contact her.

CHAPTER 4

Action outcomes and workshops: case studies

The action outcomes presented here, *Play in the Terraces*, the *Skills Exchange*, and the *Parents Centre*, emerged from the ALP learning programmes discussed in Chapter 3. Each has a very different character and has succeeded in involving a large number of people, retaining their commitment over an extended period, and creating a new kind of service based on principles of mutuality and self-help. They demonstrate the ALP approach to action, which is proactive rather than simply reactive, and is always preceded and accompanied by reflection. The ALP workers are involved at the beginning of the process in planning, and later in training and support roles.

The two workshops presented are the Writers Workshop and the Photo Workshop. Both grew out of an early phase of experimentation involving the use of ALP methods with groups based on common interests. Both are co-operatives, and embody ALP values in their ways of organizing as well as in their approach to learning.

Play in the Terraces 1982–83

When the learning programmes growing out of the Living in Gorgie Dalry investigation ended, a new group was set up to identify issues for action. These were housing density, traffic danger to children, and lack of play space. Themes emerging from discussion of these issues were personal freedom versus communal responsibility, the powerlessness of individuals to affect the behaviour of others, and the desire for privacy versus the desire to be part of a lively community. The deeper, underlying theme was named as *dependence and independence*.

A sub-group of women with small children living in the Shandon Terraces decided to explore the possibility (along with their neighbours) of tackling the conflict of interest between traffic and children's play as it affected them.

Their aims were modest: to get a play street sign erected at the entrance to the Terraces, and some double yellow lines at street corners to prevent parking and improve visibility; and to increase residents' awareness of the problem and get informal co-operation going. They knew there could be no perfect solutions, since many residents had cars and wanted to park them close to their homes. There was already tension between car owners and parents with children, and they wanted to avoid exacerbating this. Above all, they had no wish to become known as trouble-makers: they had to continue to live in the Terraces.

It was decided, therefore, not to opt for a confrontational campaign, posing children against cars, but to involve as many neighbours as possible, get the support of the local councillors, and consult highway officials and the police before any public meetings were held.

Following their initial consultations, they interviewed a cross-section of neighbours, including children, in some depth. They wanted to discover what people liked and disliked about living in the Terraces, what they felt about the tension between kids and cars, and what their suggestions were for improving the situation. About 35 people were interviewed, in an area of 330 households.

The interviews revealed that people had chosen to live in the Terraces because it was a close community. There were indeed tensions between car owners and children, and between older and younger adult residents. There was a fear that by trying to improve matters, they might be made worse. For example, residents living around the square in the centre of the Terraces did not like the suggestion that part of the square currently used as a car park might be given over to children's play. Those living further away from the square did not like the idea of their terrace being made into a play street and having to park their cars out of sight. There was a general tendency to want to shift the problem on, away from one's own front door.

Mention was made of the nearby Harrison Park as a place for children to play. Parents with grown-up children recalled that they had always played there. Parents of young children were reluctant to send their children to the park, because of the danger involved in crossing a busy main road, the absence of supervision in the park, and the danger of getting worms from dog's dirt.

This initial phase lasted from November 1981 until March 1982. An issue around was that the three key participants in the campaign felt anxious about the fact that they were playing such prominent roles. The more the word got around the area, the more anxious they became about proceeding to the next step. They had never done anything like this before. This confirmed for the ALP worker involved the correctness of the decision not to adopt a confrontational approach. Her role was to offer the women consistent support, hold them to the task, but not push them further than they felt able to go.

In May 1982, a booklet called 'Play in the Terraces', written and illustrated by the three women, was distributed to all 330 houses, giving the results of the investigation. Their introduction made it clear that, although their prime concern was to get play made safer

22. Boys playing on bikes in the Terraces

23. Play in the Terraces campaign – open-air display

for children, they continued to be aware of the needs of other residents. The booklet contained facts and figures about parking and the numbers of children in different age groups living in the area; quotes from interviews with residents, identifying some of the tensions revealed; a sketch of the park as redesigned by a 10-year-old girl; a history of the Terraces; sketches of children's street games; proposals from residents for improving the situation; and comments from officials. It ended with an invitation to attend a public meeting early in June.

Three days before the public meeting, a caravan display was set up in the central square with photographs of street life in the Terraces taken by a member of the Photo Workshop, and flip charts on which those residents who had not been interviewed could write their comments. This open air event was well attended, and videotaped by a resident.

The public meeting attracted over 60 people. It was organized as a 'problemat' workshop, in which people were invited to say what their vision was for improving play in the Terraces, what the blocks were, and how they might be overcome.

In British culture, the tradition at public meetings is that those who call them are expected to have clear proposals to put to those who attend them. The role of the floor of the meeting is to discuss the proposals from the platform and then vote on them. It took some time for residents who attended this meeting to accept that the campaign leaders wanted to engage in dialogue with other participants. Like everyone else they had brought along their own ideas, but they saw their role as helping everyone's ideas to emerge, enabling full discussion to take place, and working towards achieving a consensus.

Twenty people joined a working party to take things further, with the help of local councillors. The working party met three times to thrash out proposals to put to the Highways, Leisure and Recreation, and Environmental Health Committees of the council. These included double yellow lines, sleeping policemen (bumps in the road to cut down speed), a clean-up of the park, and the appointment of a park keeper. The more radical proposals (e.g. for zoning parts of the Terraces for kids or cars) were rejected. On the whole residents preferred informal arrangements to prevail.

Finally, in February 1983, a second booklet was distributed to residents, bringing them up to date on what had been achieved: double yellow lines and a clean-up and zoning of the park, with a separate area for dogs. Later, sections of the main road through the Terraces were raised and cobbled. Perhaps the most important achievement was to bring the issue to the forefront of residents' awareness, and to increase communication and informal co-operation about it.

Tit for Tat: the Skills Exchange 1982–87

Like Play in the Terraces, the Skills Exchange grew out of the work of a group formed at the end of the first learning programmes. The issue was unemployment and its effects on the individual and on family relationships. It was summed up by a woman whose husband had just lost his job:

> When you're unemployed, you're on your own completely. Even though others are in the same boat, you've lost your framework. There is nothing you *have* to do. There is nothing *for* you to do. And you know you won't starve.

She felt sorry for him, but he was getting under her feet at home. The underlying theme was dependence and independence. In exploring it, the group became aware of a striking contradiction, that whilst there were lots of workers in Gorgie Dalry, whose skills were rusting away for lack of use, there were others, also unemployed or on low incomes, who couldn't afford to get essential jobs done.

In October 1981, a suggestion was made for setting up a barter system. A member of the group described how she had been given a bag of potatoes in exchange for the use of her washing machine. The group wondered if this idea could be extended to exchanges of jobs involving the use of people's skills. One of the ALP workers was asked to find out more about barter, and discovered the existence of skills exchanges, one called Network in Liverpool, and others in the USA where the idea was highly developed and commercialized.

There followed an intense period of discussion in the group about the different types of skills exchange, the principles which would underpin the one proposed for Gorgie Dalry, and the way it would operate. The key principle – addressing the theme of dependence and independence – was to be mutuality. The notion of credits for jobs done was considered and dismissed. It was decided to rely on the simpler notion of a bank or register of skills on which members could draw according to need. Fears were expressed about people abusing the system by getting lots of jobs done and never giving anything in return. There were also fears about jobs being botched because of lack of skill or commitment. It was decided to go ahead in spite of these fears, and rely on negotiation between members. If a member felt she was being asked to do too many jobs, she could say no. The person wanting the job done could check out with the person offering to do it if he had the skills required. The skills exchange itself would not guarantee quality. It would function as a co-operative, with the ALP shop as contact point and meeting place, where members would come together regularly and get to know each other. Its foundation would be trust and interdependence.

The Skills Exchange was publicized and launched in January 1982, with the name Tit for Tat. It was open to everyone living in the area, not just the unemployed. Over 100 members joined within three months. There were regular core group meetings, and larger gatherings of members, with a high rate of exchanges going on. It was a simple idea with a ready appeal. It became widely known, and for a while ALP *was* the Skills Exchange.

Here is how it worked. There was a card for each member, giving name, address, and telephone number, occupation (if any), and skills offered. On the back of the card, a record was kept of jobs the member had done. There was a separate card for each skill, with a list of members who could perform it, so cross-referencing was easy. A diary was kept of new members joining, jobs requested, and jobs done. Once a week, members of the core group came into the ALP shop to keep the records up to date, and start the exchange process. The member requesting a job was given the name and telephone number of those offering that skill: the rest was up to them. No money changed hands. Materials required for the job had to be provided by the recipient. One partner in the exchange informed the shop when the job had been done, so that it could be recorded in the diary and listed in the newsletter. A monthly review was held to identify which jobs had been done, and which were still outstanding.

Skills offered included home decorating, basic joinery, typing, making and mending clothes, weeding, window box skills, car maintenance, French, German, Gaelic, Russian, English 'O' grade and Higher, help with letter writing, CV preparation and job interview practice, babysitting, small pet sitting, ironing, driving tuition, shopping and going to the library for the housebound, shiatsu massage, bicycle maintenance, singing, computing, baking, dog walking, furniture removal, physics, chemistry, numeracy, snooker, conversation, completing DHSS forms, counselling, advice on nutrition, reading to blind people, architectural advice, graphic design, and help with book-keeping and VAT. There were many more.

An important part of the life of the Skills Exchange was its regular socials. These were open to all members and took place in the ALP Shop, with music-making, poetry-reading and pot-luck suppers. Through the socials, members got to know each other and found it easier to ask someone to do a job for them. These occasions were often used as platforms for individual members to demonstrate their skill, and for recruiting members to small learning exchanges. Members of the Skills Exchange were often also members of other ALP groups, and for a time the socials functioned as the heart of the whole project. Here is what one unemployed member said about the Skills exchange to a researcher:

> I was surprised by the range of skills on offer: everything from plumbing to psychiatry! For an unemployed person like myself, it's marvellous to have an alternative to the usual way of doing things which can be prohibitively expensive. But the Skills Exchange is not charity. Everyone is contributing their own time and talents for the benefit of the group, so its not a case of getting something for nothing. As well as the obvious immediate benefits – getting things done or learning how to do them – the experience of being in the Skills Exchange is good for me in other ways. I am learning how to work with other people, and to be part of a group which doesn't rely on the old methods of bosses and underlings to be effective. It's also a lot of fun and has allowed me to meet lots of people I would certainly never have encountered had I spent all my time on the dole hanging around feeling depressed.

But there were problems. Some members felt the system was inefficient. Others felt it was too structured. The core group consisted of enthusiastic volunteers, with other members required to serve on it for a short period when their names came up on the rota. Key members would often invest enormous amounts of time and energy in running and developing the Skills Exchange, then move on, sometimes to paid employment or further education. The net result was lack of continuity.

In order to feel part of the Skills Exchange, members had to be asked to do jobs. But some skills were more in demand than others. Some members were never asked to do a job, and just slipped away.

A lot of energy was expended on encouraging members to ask for jobs to be done, but there was simply never enough demand. A connected problem was that those who had not themselves been asked to do a job were reluctant to ask for a job to be done for them. And all members were reluctant to ask for really big jobs, feeling that those ought to be paid for.

A system of key members in each sub-area of Gorgie Dalry was created, whose task was to keep in touch with members living near them by delivering the newsletter and encouraging people to come to general meetings and socials. But this did not solve the problem of lack of demand.

Finally, our adherence to the principle of mutuality prevented one possible avenue of growth from opening up. Requests were received from voluntary organizations, social workers, and community centres to provide volunteer tutors and jobbers. These were refused on the grounds that they would undermine the principle of mutuality, and turn the Skills Exchange into a Volunteer Bureau.

In 1984, a part-time worker was appointed for a few months to find ways of maximizing the involvement of members, and to see if the Skills Exchange could be made independent of ALP. The level of activity and enthusiasm rose during this period, but the attempts to obtain independent funding from trusts failed.

After ALP's integration into Lothian Regions Community Education Service in 1985, the Skills Exchange was revived. Unemployed ALP members and students on placement set about reorganizing it as the voluntary wing of the project. Swop nights were started. These were meetings held every two months to generate exchanges between members, and ideas for learning groups. They were also social events, each with a theme reflecting the season of the year.

A group was set up to run short courses tutored by skills exchange members, and open to anyone in the area. Courses so far have included sewing, first aid, bicycle maintenance, astrology, people and health, massage, and assertiveness. Another popular aspect of the revamped Skills Exchange is the tradition of weekend cook-ins in the ALP Shop, where members demonstrate how to cook their favourite dishes.

The Skills Exchange is a powerful idea, whose potential has been demonstrated, but not yet fully realized. Further experiments in this direction are needed.

The Parents Centre 1986–87

The Parents Centre grew out of the learning programme about bringing up children in different cultures. The theme was identified *as excessive individualism* or *group conformity* versus *co-operation out of one's own authority and identity*. In people's lives, the theme cashed out as feelings of isolation, a heavy burden of responsibility, and a desire for more support.

A decision was made to explore the possibility of setting up a family centre where parents could meet and benefit from each others's experience. Starting in January 1986, a core group of 16 parents and an ALP worker began the feasibility study. While protracted negotiations about a possible venue were proceeding, there was time to work out in advance members' vision of the proposed centre, its underlying principles, how it might be organized, and anticipate some of the problems likely to arise.

The vision was for a welcoming place where it would be possible to be honest and share with other parents one's limitations as a parent, with structured activities and learning programmes taking place away from the children, and with a creche where new members could stay with their children until they settled, and their parents felt ready to join a group.

The emphasis would be on growth rather than problems. Worries could be aired and support given to individuals, but the main purpose would be to allow parents to learn from each other and from sympathetic professionals. As in the Skills Exchange, mutuality was the underlying principle.

There was a wish to keep the organization simple and avoid too many committee meetings. The ALP worker challenged the group to imagine themselves already running the centre. What would they need to talk about at committee meetings? How would the other members hear about the decisions? How would the centre reach out to other parents in the community? What support would the centre require?

Group members' responses revealed contradictions in their thinking. Some felt that if the centre was to be called a family centre, it might exclude the elderly, single people, and childless couples. There was a wish not to be exclusive. But if everyone was to be included, what was to be the focus? The group decided to focus on people involved in parenting, but others (elderly people for example) could be drawn in to help run the creche or take part in a rent-a-granny scheme.

Another contradiction was the plan to elect a committee but involve everyone in making all the decisions. A third contradiction concerned making allowances for parents of very young children. Members felt that new parents needed to be allowed to be dependent, but also had to be encouraged to take responsibility. It would be important to avoid a divide between providers and consumers.

The group began to worry about taking on too much. The fear was that they would have to commit too much time to the project. It was agreed that reliability rather than quantity of time was the crucial factor. But behind this worry about time lay anxiety about taking on additional responsibility. One parent complained:

I need a support system for myself. I don't need more responsibility.

Another responded:

That's the contradiction. Your situation is the reason we want to set up a family centre in the first place. But for you to get the kind of support you're talking about, we need to provide something that brings people together.

Whilst these discussions were going on, individual volunteers and the ALP worker were finding out about existing family centres. Their research showed that most family centres were child-centred. The group decided that their centre would focus primarily on the needs of parents. To signal this therefore, they changed the proposed name to the Parents Centre.

By March, the group had reached agreement about the kind of centre they wanted. Negotiations with the first possible venue had ended in failure. St Bride's Community Centre was approached and agreement was reached to locate the Parents Centre there.

It opened in September 1986, meeting one morning a week for two hours, with structured programmes of activity and discussion, co-ordinated by members and with resource people providing expertise.

Since then, programmes have been offered each term always including elements of activity and discussion. Topics have included: kids and confrontation, individual identity and one's role as a parent, living with teenagers, the influence of books and television on our children, problems in the transition between home and school, sibling rivalry and parental favouritism, feeding children, preventing accidents, and the function of play.

Activity sessions have included: moving and stretching to music, basic yoga positions with emphasis on relaxation, foot massage for all the family, home remedies for children's accidents, drama workshops in movement and mime, and drama workshops enacting issues in parenting.

Numbers are limited by the amount of space available and the capacity of the creche which is limited to 20 children. The number of parents registered as members is 28, with an average attendance at sessions of 20.

Organization meetings are held once a term to sort out problems and plan the following term's programmes. The centre is supported by an ALP worker and by the manager of St Bride's Community Centre. It has succeeded in attracting new members, including several fathers, and has achieved the ambition of its founders that it should become a place of both stimulation and support for parents: more than a mother and toddler group.

Gorgie Dalry Writers Workshop 1981–87

The Writers Workshop was started by one of the ALP workers in September 1981. It was felt that writing would be an important way for people to explore significant themes. Saying your own word, could be interpreted as writing your own word.

The worker began by inviting people to write at home on matters of concern. Work was read out in the group, and during the discussion which followed, the worker would tentatively name the themes emerging. These were found to be particular to each writer. Each member's background was different, and it was difficult to draw the threads together and identify a theme common to the group as a whole. Further, there was a reluctance to discuss personal themes, and a tendency to see disagreement about the content of a piece of writing as criticism of it as writing. It was quickly recognized that ALP's initial expectation was inappropriate.

Those joining the Writers Workshop had in common an interest in writing as a form of creativity and expression. They wanted to share their work with other writers, get criticism and support, improve their technique, build up their confidence, and eventually perform their work in public. They also saw workshop meetings as opportunities to socialize: part two generally took place in the Auld Worthies pub across the road.

As time went on, it was realized that themes did emerge, but that the process was very different from that in a decoding group or a learning programme. The theme would be contained in an individual piece of writing, which resonated with other members, leading them to pick it up and write about it in response.

The workshop met weekly during the evening, in the ALP Shop. It was open to anyone in the area and beyond. Numbers attending varied from 6 to over 20: a normal attendance would be anything from 10 to 15.

ALP principles showed up strongly in the organization of the Writers Workshop. It was run as a co-operative, with members taking it in turns to co-ordinate and record the meeting. Programmes were planned in advance and there were regular review sessions. There was a willingness to experiment in the structure of sessions and in a variety of methods used to stimulate writing and criticism.

24. The Writers Workshop – a demonstration session

The ethos of the Writers Workshop can be summed up as follows: a commitment to openness and informality; anti-elitism with a degree of anti-expert and anti-authority feeling; a preference for support rather than challenge, and spontaneity rather than structure.

From the earliest days, the Writers Workshop has been involved in publishing its members' work, giving performances at various festivals and linking up with other writers workshops throughout Scotland and the north of England to build the Writers Workshop movement.

Although fiercely independent in its decision making and style of working, the Writers Workshop is a member of the ALP Association with a long history of effective contributions to the life of the project as a whole. Writers Workshop members were among the first to attend workshops to train group co-ordinators run by ALP staff. They have contributed to many of ALP's celebrations through their readings and performances. They were prominent in the campaign to save ALP and helped to write the campaign documents. The workshop retains its link with ALP through representation on the co-ordinating group, and the attendance of an ALP worker at its quarterly review meetings.

The workshop has had its ups and downs over the past seven years. It is currently going strong. A new member joining now would find that the meetings are organized in a four-weekly cycle, as follows: reading and criticism session: stimulus and writing in the group; more reading and criticism; public performance and planning of festival contributions. Each month there is one additional session, when Gorgie Dalry joins with other writers workshops to put on a poems and pints night in a city pub.

The Photo Workshop 1982–87

Photography has always been central to the ALP project, partly because one of the workers is a trained photographer, and partly because it was decided early on that photography was a good medium for making codifications. Like writing, it was seen as a way in which people could say their own word, in the sense of making a visual statement about some aspect of the world.

In June 1982, the first ALP social documentary project started. An advertisement invited unemployed people with an interest in photography to join a group which would take photographs for the project in return for a free supply of film. The ALP worker explained what a codification was, ran a decoding session, described the themes emerging from earlier learning programmes, and sent members out to take photographs to illustrate these in their own way. The agreement was that the photographers could keep as many prints as they wanted, within reason, but that the negatives belonged to the project. The ALP worker and group members constructed a darkroom in the old boiler-room of St Martin's Church. Several went on to get jobs in photography, or joined full-time training courses.

The next phase in the development of photography in ALP was the formal constitution of the Photo Workshop in September 1983.

It began to hold regular Monday meetings, mounted its first exhibition, and reprinted old photographs for the Living Memory project. The emphasis shifted from social documentary work to building an organization with a programme accommodating a wide range of interests, of which social documentary was one.

In May 1985 a highly productive phase began, with another round of social documentary projects involving unemployed people. Money was found to pay one of the workshop members as a tutor to co-ordinate the building up of a photo archive which would attempt to record all aspects of life in Gorgie Dalry, and be a ready source of codifications for use in ALP learning programmes.

The standard of photography was improving all the time, and the degree of tension over who owned the negatives was also rising. At this stage the Photo Workshop, of which the unemployed social documentary group was a part, mounted a number of major public exhibitions, including 'Saturday in Gorgie Dalry'.

In the spring of 1986, work began on building a new darkroom and studio in premises at 4b Downfield Place, next door to the ALP Shop. This was to be developed as a community photography resource. It was funded by Photo Workshop members' subscriptions, and grants from Edinburgh District Council, Lothian Regional Council and the Scottish Arts Council. A big recruitment drive resulted in a change in the membership profile of the Workshop, with more members now in employment. The effect was to make it in some ways more stable as a group, with access to more resources, but a group in which the commitment of some members was less intense than when it consisted mainly of unemployed people. The new members tended to see photography more as a leisure-time activity and less as a full-time passion. The ALP worker concerned feels strongly that the involvement of at least 25 per cent of unemployed members makes all the difference to the seriousness of the workshop.

The first major exhibition to be mounted by the workshop out of its new premises was 'Tenement Life', which was presented as part of Edinburgh District Council's Spring Fling festival in 1987, to which Gorgie Dalry Writers Workshop contributed a play on the same theme.

The belief held by the Photo Workshop is that the best way to learn photography is to work alone or with others, on projects which have a clear direction and endpoint, rather than simply snapping at random.

Anyone joining the Photo Workshop at the time of writing will find themselves involved in a varied programme. There is a monthly cycle of meetings including a session on planning projects and exhibitions, practical teaching in the darkroom or in the studio, assessing members' prints, and discussing a guest photographer's portfolio. At other times, new members may be involved in mounting exhibitions in community centres, cafes, or festival venues, producing photographs for ALP learning programmes, local drama productions, the community newspaper and other voluntary organizations. Or they might be invited to join the small group of social documentary photographers currently involved in ALP's newest investigation into Living with Change in Gorgie Dalry. As their skill increases, they will find themselves involved in teaching less experienced members, either informally in the darkroom, or in short courses in basic photography open to anyone who is interested.

Members are encouraged to contribute to the organization of the Photo Workshop, which also sends a representative to the ALP co-ordinating group, and benefits from the regular support of an ALP worker.

Since its inception, members of the Photo Workshop have supplied a great number of high quality images for use in decoding sessions and learning programmes. A number of individual photographers have collaborated closely with members of learning groups, giving technical advice on how to produce their own codifications, or receiving briefs for the creation of images designed to express the groups' themes. When this dialogue between photographers and participants has been established, it has always been creative.

Action outcomes and workshops: issues arising

- ALP action outcomes and workshops have tended not to adopt a confrontational style, and in this respect represent a departure from the tradition of the 1960s and 1970s. This has arisen partly from circumstances – there has been no pressure for confrontational campaigns – partly from ALP's ideological commitment to dialogue, and partly from the workers' conviction, from their own experiences of confrontational styles, that they have limited effect on the situation, and sometimes harm participants. Having said that, ALP recognizes the need for confrontation in desperate circumstances if it is considered to be the most effective, or only, strategy available.

- ALP depends on co-operation, dialogue, and commitment to the task of the group. But the workshops, which are essentially interest groups, attract into membership creative people motivated by self-interest. They want access to services, a chance to develop their creativity, and personal kudos. For some, participation in a group is secondary and very much a means to other ends. This is an issue for every group and every person, and relates to the theme, highlighted by ALP, of being-for-self and being-for-others. It is a tension which individuals and groups have to work at.

- A balance has to be achieved between investing ALP workers' time in new investigations and learning programmes, and in support for action outcomes and workshops. In practice, learning programmes must have priority, and support for outcomes must therefore be limited.

- There is a big investment of worker time in learning programmes and in preparation for action. Thereafter, worker involvement is reduced to giving support to group leaders, and attending the quarterly review meetings of the whole group. The issue here is: how can the ALP ethos be maintained and renewed? Experienced members eventually move on, and new people join who have not taken part in learning programmes or in the struggle to create the organizations. The net effect can be a dilution of the ALP ideology and an increase in the influence of other ideologies in the culture, for example, consumerist attitudes, the expectations that a service will be provided, passivity in the learning process, reluctance to take responsibility, an emphasis on enjoyment and support, a dislike of hard work and challenge, and a preference for expression rather than reflection and new knowledge. On the other hand, new members bring in fresh energy, new ways of seeing, new ideas, and new hopes. The issue becomes one of holding on to a core, and encouraging new growth. It involves regeneration, which requires good leadership.

- Given the limited time the two ALP workers can devote to the action outcomes and workshops, leadership has to come from the members, and be self-renewing. In ALP, the most committed volunteers have tended to be the unemployed, housewives and retired people, with time and mental energy to spare. But when they leave or move on to another stage in their lives, the ethos can leave with them if new people have not been trained up to take their place.

CHAPTER 5

The influence of ALP

In order to be able to give a reasonably accurate impression of the project's influence as it has unfolded over the years, the workers have carried out interviews with participants at various stages, and kept records of the training events they have organized and the consultations they have been involved in.

The general theme is discussed in the following sequence: influence on participants, influence on ALP staff themselves, and influence on fellow professionals and voluntary workers in adult and community education.

Influence on participants

During the period 1979–87, a total of 97 interviews with participants in ALP have been carried out by ALP staff, Open University researchers, the project's external assessors, placement students, and part-time researchers. The following analysis is based mainly on the records of 37 interviews carried out in February 1981, August 1984, and August 1987. Of the 37 people interviewed 11 were male and 26 female. 21 were married (19 with children), 2 were divorced (both with children) 3 were widowed (1 with children), and 11 were single. Age distribution was: 13 in their twenties; 15 in their thirties; 5 in their forties, and 1 each in their fifties, sixties, seventies, and eighties. 20 were in full or part-time employment, 7 were unemployed, 7 were housewives, and 3 were retired.

In selecting people for interview, ALP attempted to choose a cross-section of those involved in the project at any one time, but with preference given to those participating in more than one ALP programme.

Influence is an elusive quality. Much of it is invisible to the researcher, and some is unknown to the subject. No matter how sensitive the interviewer and how attentive to nuances of verbal and non-verbal communication, what is gained is inevitably a subjective impression. Subjective impressions are not regarded in ALP as lacking in validity, and particularly when impressions begin to accumulate and patterns emerge from a number of interviews carried out by different interviewers, it is reasonable to assume that a significant theme has been identified. That is the method used in analysing these 37 records. The themes have been placed in a sequence that broadly reflects the stages of the ALP process.

The question of longer and shorter-term influence is more difficult. About half of those interviewed had had a considerable period of involvement (over two years) in ALP and had experienced a variety of ALP programmes at the time of interview. The other half were commenting on experiences of shorter-term duration.

Recruitment

ALP appeared to attract people who were going through transitions in their lives, either changes in their external circumstances, or their relationships, or in their images of themselves. This theme was most often expressed by young mothers at home or by unemployed people. One woman, referring to issues being discussed in the Women and Well-being programme said: I was thinking a lot about these things and noting a change in myself. ALP speeded up the process.

First impressions

Many of those interviewed said they had no idea what ALP was about when they started. First impressions had been important in holding people's attention until they could begin to understand. Individuals referred to the enthusiasm of the ALP workers, the warm, convivial atmosphere in the shop, the fact that everyone seemed prepared to listen. Others spoke of having been accepted as they were and of being encouraged to explore their interest in art or photography in a practical way before being invited to join a learning group:

I'd walked past the ALP Shop a hundred times and thought, 'bloody education – I hate teachers!' I was living in a dump at the time and I'd no job. I hated bosses, too! Then one day I saw an advert in the window inviting unemployed people to learn about social documentary photography. It was free. I didn't want a class. I wanted to learn about photography by taking pictures. Before I knew it I was in Orwell School taking pictures of the kids for the campaign to keep the school open. I liked the idea of taking pictures of something useful. Then I found I was being asked what I *thought*. That's how it all started.

Saying what you think

Several people admitted they were alarmed at being asked to contribute to discussion in learning groups right from the start. They felt sure no-one would be interested in their views or hearing about their experiences. When they did risk speaking, they were delighted to be taken seriously. This was often their most enduring impression of an ALP group:

Everyone participates in the discussion.

You find yourself talking openly to people you wouldn't normally meet.

You say things you only thought before.

You hear yourself and others in the group.

Listening and re-presenting

This climate of active listening and the worker's role in encouraging it was referred to by many interviewees. They talked about the effect of a worker re-presenting members' contributions to the group:

It's good to be able to say something unintelligible and get it spoken back to you in a way you and everybody else can understand. It gives you the chance to adjust it, explain further, or say yep, that's it!

Learning from others

One interviewee explained the effect dialogue had on him:

Usually in life you have very fixed viewpoints. You'll have this standpoint and you'll stick to it no matter what, and if it's proved wrong you'll try to find ways of making it look right instead of accepting that you're wrong. In ALP there's a constant shift in position. Say at one stage you had this stance and someone comes up with X information, you realize you're wrong and you make some steps towards their stance. It's all sort of built up slowly.

Discussions in ALP were said to have an equalizing effect. Those who left school early discovered they knew more than they thought they did. Those with more education realized the limitations of what they knew.

Feeling different

Participants often carried on the discussion at home, but some found the climate unwelcoming.

Sometimes it's made me feel further away from friends because it's difficult to explain what we've been doing and they don't understand how excited I am, whereas before everyone was just content to talk about kids and everything like that. They don't understand what it's all about. It's only recently that I've been beginning to understand how to explain it to myself.

Taking responsibility

One woman said:

In ALP groups you grow together and get support. You're treated as an adult and expected to take the responsibility as an adult. If you're in the group, it's part of your responsibility to choose which way the group goes.

Anticipating her first learning programme, another woman said:

We're going to choose what we learn. It's not a laid-down course. We can say we want to learn ABCD instead of a teacher saying you're *going* to learn EFGH.

At the end of a learning programme people realized they were confronted with the possibility of 'acting on your thinking', as someone put it. She understood the choice was hers. In her case it meant being active in the Play in the Terraces campaign, putting her in the limelight where she had no wish to be.

Leading a group

The challenge interviewees said they resisted longest, was the invitation to lead a learning or action group. They felt they didn't have sufficient skill or authority to do the job. They were reluctant to stand out from the crowd and risk the disapproval of fellow members or neighbours.

Teaching and learning

Some interviewees found themselves thinking more critically about the relationships between teachers and students in classes or groups. The women who attended a photography class at night school spoke of having to wait their turn for the teacher's attention. There was no attempt to use the students' experience for the benefit of other students. She compared this with the co-operative nature of ALP's Photo Workshop where participants were used as co-educators and got more done as a result.

Another woman, who had attended a Women's Health group before joining the ALP Women and Well-being programme, described it as 'Just a chat with no new information'.

But whenever interviewees found themselves in a formal educational setting where tutors were experimenting with different methods, they were quick to appreciate it, and very supportive of the tutor's efforts. One woman, who was attending a refresher course for nursery nurses at the local F.E. college, spoke enthusiastically about the tutor negotiating the programme on the basis of students' experience and their need to know more.

Action

People were clear about the role of reflection in ensuring effective action in ALP groups. Six years after the creation of the Skills Exchange, interviewees recalled in detail the way it had emerged from discussion and how, once action was underway, time was spent on carefully working out policy.

Similarly, in discussing the Play in the Terraces campaign, references were made to the reasonable approach of asking people about their experience of the issues, keeping them informed, involving as many people as possible in decision-making, and not trying to force proposals through where there was no general agreement. This enabled the activists to feel all right about their nerve in starting the campaign in the first place:

> It made me feel very determined that no matter how uncomfortable it was I would always be able to do hard things if they were right.

A leading participant in the campaign to save ALP, who was a disillusioned trade unionist and political activist, said that ALP had restored his faith in action. He described the approach:

> First you learn to listen to another person's point of view and become better able to put your own. Action follows from searching out the resources and people willing to help, and building up a case. It's not about waving banners in the air.

Applying the lessons of ALP

Interviewees, including some who had not been involved in ALP for several years, found it easy to say how they had applied the lessons of ALP in other areas of their lives. As one man put it:

> It isn't just about education. ALP learning is about life. It's getting through your daily life learning to deal with people in a more reasonable way. It's listening to others and being flexible enough to change the belief you've been carrying around in your head.

There were examples from personal life, including encouraging your child to ask more questions at school; negotiating a change of school; organizing a stair meeting to get repairs done; and going for job interviews. There were examples from the work setting: the lab technician who encouraged students to look for a variety of solutions to problems; the playgroup worker who was setting up a business and didn't get so frustrated when she didn't achieve her ideal immediately; the hospital nurse who now voiced her opinion and valued her own judgement and had stopped thinking that other people had all the knowledge and she didn't have any; the community arts organizer who knew from his experience of running ALP groups how much work he needed to put in to create the informal effect in a group; the part-time art tutor who used decoding and re-presentation to get students to think about things in a different way. She did not give answers but encouraged her students to think things out for themselves.

A sheltered life?

Interviewees spoke of the need for support for the ALP approach in the organization in which they were trying to operate. This was sometimes present and sometimes not. A woman found support for her attempts to take a leading role in church meetings:

> I trust people. I've learned to listen. I'm not afraid to speak up if I disagree with what's being said. I ask questions and try to get other people involved. People see what I'm trying to do and they support me.

Another woman was less fortunate. In her organization the emphasis was all on action. The committee did not seem to see the need for reflection or sometimes even for agendas or minutes. She said she felt she had led a 'sheltered life' in ALP. It was difficult to stand out against the organization's set way of doing things. However, at a moment of crisis in the life of the organization, she was able to codify the problem as she saw it in the form of a diagram, and encourage dialogue around it.

A part-time youth worker in a community centre was also struggling. He felt that the ALP approach required support and 'a gradual learning together in a give-and-take situation'. Neither of these were available to him, and as a part-timer he felt there was little he could do to improve matters.

Conclusion

In conclusion interviewees seemed to have taken from ALP what they needed most, whether it was intellectual stimulation, emotional support or friendship. They spoke of their growing self-confidence and respect for themselves as adults. They had been offered things they had not expected or even wanted: the chance to become leaders, to become more aware of the contributions of others, to be more reflective, to act on their thinking, and to be more realistic in their ambitions. Finally, they got a range of training opportunities.

Training participants

ALP had always been committed to making its philosophy and methodology explicit and available to participants. Understanding the process in which they were involved and how it could be used in other aspects of their lives was an important part of what ALP members learned. But they were also encouraged to use it in a much more immediate way in their leadership of ALP groups. Their need became acute when, at the end of a learning programme which had been worker-led, they moved into the action phase, which could, of course, involve further learning programmes run by members themselves.

At this point, ALP offered support through the apprenticeship system. A worker met with those who had volunteered to co-ordinate the group in advance, to brainstorm the content of the programme, to work out the structure, identify useful resource people, and agree the division of labour between the volunteers. Thereafter the worker met them regularly to talk about any problems they were experiencing. At the end of term the worker met the whole group, including the leaders, to talk about how it had gone both in terms of content and process.

Once a year a training programme was offered to anyone in ALP wanting to develop leadership skills. It included members of different ALP groups, some with a lot of experience of leadership and others who were fairly new to the task. Cross-fertilization was an important feature of such training groups. Educational and organizational issues were tackled.

The worker might give a short presentation on particular skills, for example, structuring a session, getting through a business agenda, or asking open questions in a discussion group. The dialogue which developed was based on an exchange of participants' difficulties in practice and their pressing anxieties. The worker and other more experienced members responded to questions with practical suggestions. Individuals might use the occasion to prepare for a session. An example of this was the two women who worked out how they were going to structure a meeting of the Parents' Association at their children's school the following week.

Another example of training was the work done with church house groups. The priest of St Martin's Episcopal Church invited an ALP worker in to help train group leaders. House groups are church members meeting in each other's homes to explore the implications of their basic Christian beliefs for their everyday lives. A key point to note here is the collaboration between ALP and another local institution, in which the project adapted its methods to the task of the institution.

Influence on the ALP workers

Fiona, Stan and Gerri all felt excited about getting a chance to put Paulo Freire's ideas into action. Certain key words struck home and had a deep influence: cointentionality, dialogue, themes and contradictions. What would it mean in practice to be a dialogical educator?

Adapting Freire's ideas gave them a basic structure and set of methods for their work. But it was more than an approach to adult education, it was a way of seeing and a way of relating to other people, which they were keen to share. Over the years it has become integrated into their personalities, and has had spill-over effects into other aspects of their lives.

The experience of leading groups was a source of energy. Being part of a team gave inspiration, discipline and support. The training role was a source of renewal, because they relearned the difficult ideas in the process of explaining them to others. They positively enjoyed the fact that participants could have a clear expectation of them in their role as workers, and that they in turn could make their expectations of participants clear.

For most of her period with the project Fiona lived in the area. She says that ALP changed her life and taught her what education was all about. It gave her new skills and increased her confidence. She knows *why* she's doing things. This may appear as arrogance, but it isn't that. In her new work situation, a community centre in a peripheral housing scheme, she is continuing to adapt ALP ideas. ALP has helped her to hang on to her basic optimism.

Stan's wife thinks he is a different father to his children from what he might have been if he hadn't got involved in ALP. He feels that ALP has helped him to become interested in processes as well as in goals. It has confirmed his belief that salvation lies in having an active relationship to life. People in the audience learn less, he thinks. Gerri thinks his attitudes to experts and to authority have changed. He now sees a clearer place for new knowledge in the learning process (he has long recognized the importance of experience).

Gerri feels that Freire and ALP have given her a structure and shield against the chaos of the kind of community work she had previously experienced, and restored some of her idealism. Stan and Fiona both remember her as world-weary at the beginning of the project. As time has gone on, she feels she has become more realistic and tolerant, and increased her capacity for spontaneity.

It could be said that all three set out with excessively high hopes for these exciting ideas, and an overwhelming sense of their own responsibility as educators. Now they are more realistic and more relaxed. But they find the ideas as integrating and stimulating as ever.

Influence on fellow professionals

This influence has been exercised through ALP's approach to training and consultation, which is based on Freire's concept of co-education. A selection of initiatives is presented to give some flavour of this strand of the work.

The Freire in Britain seminar

In June 1984 fifty participants came to Pollock Halls in Edinburgh for a two-day residential workshop. They included fieldworkers in adult and community education, community schools, church work, and mental health projects, from Scotland, England and Northern Ireland. Among them was a Chilean refugee who had been trained as a monitor by Freire.

Papers on Freire's ideas and the ALP process were sent out in advance, and participants were asked to think about issues in their own practice. The sessions included presentations on the process, small group discussion relating theory to practice, experiential workshops on investigation, decoding and programme-building, and dialogues with members of ALP groups.

The Practitioners' Skills Exchange

Out of this seminar grew an idea for a supportive network of practitioners in Lothian Region who were working directly with learning groups. The result was the creation, in December 1984, of the Practititioners' Skills Exchange, modelled on ALP's own skills exchange, and based on the idea of give-and-take between experienced workers. The original invitation was to share insights, problems and skills in a structured learning programme, drawing on additional resources as required. Those who joined included adult basic education and community school staff, mental health and community health workers, Second Chance course tutors, and the ALP workers themselves.

They met on the last Friday of each month. Attendance varied between 6 and 15 people. Members concentrated on what they had in common, namely a concern with group processes, the relationships between members, issues of leadership, how dialogue is established and used as a learning method, and how groups are maintained and developed.

The Practitioners' Skills Exchange had the same problems as any other dialogical learning group. An early issue was members dropping in and dropping out and the bad effect that had on learning. This led members to make contracts with each other to attend every monthly meeting for a set period of time, usually six months. There was a tension between structuring the programme in advance, and responding spontaneously in a supportive way to individual members who were having problems in their practice. The first programme of meetings was very structured, with one person volunteering to prepare a presentation for each session.

In the second programme, topics were planned in advance but members were to come ready to contribute from their own experience. Each took it in turn to co-ordinate the discussion. Space was left at the end of each meeting to deal with burning issues in the here and now. This was called the clinic. The great benefit of the Practitioners' Skills Exchange is that it takes people out of their immediate practice context, enabling them to talk freely yet maintain confidentiality.

For the third programme, it was decided to make a virtue of reality and accept that the Practitioners' Skills Exchange was a learning group like any other, with problems of group dynamics and group leadership. Topics were still planned in advance, but reflection on the learning experience in the group was programmed in. Someone volunteered to play the role of observer, feeding back observations of the behaviour of members and the co-ordinator during the last ten minutes of the meeting.

In the fourth programme, a list of topics was generated at the start of the contracted period of six monthly meetings. One was selected at the end of each meeting for the next. A presenter offered to lead off the discussion with illustrations from her own practice. Once more there was a clinic for burning issues at the end.

Community education workers' training

When ALP was established in 1985 part of the remit was that ALP workers would contribute to the development of adult education training for community education staff in the Region. The first offering was a theory and practice course on ALP methods. With support from team leaders and CEOs, 11 workers were recruited by networking amongst those interested in adult education group work. Participants attended initial workshops on ALP's philosophy and methodology. They then designed a piece of work appropriate to their own context and began to implement it, returning regularly to discuss it with the ALP workers and each other over a six-month period.

ALP's training for community education staff seemed most effective when workers managed to adapt certain aspects of the ALP process to their own work, for example where a community education worker used decoding to encourage part-time youth workers to think about their practice on club nights, and define their own training needs.

Collaboration with Adult Basic Education (ABE)

Lothian Region's Adult Basic Education team is the only sector of the Community Education Service solely concerned with adult education. Relations between ABE and ALP are cordial, with regular collaboration on training and in some learning projects. In the autumn of 1986 an ALP worker began to work jointly with an ABE tutor to test the feasibility of using decoding as the basis of language work along Freirean lines.

The two workers met with a small group of ABE students for two hours a week, over a period of eight weeks. The area of investigation was narrowed down to life in a large peripheral housing scheme where most participants lived. Each week the session began with a structured discussion focusing on how people experienced life in that situation. One of the key codifications was a photo of a tower block of flats, without any people in the picture. Participants spoke about it as a *concentration camp*, as *Alcatraz*. Talk then moved to the lifts, their filthy state (*junkies* shoot up in them), children's *fear* of going up alone, and the risk they take asking an unknown adult to accompany them. Adults feared attack, too. One man's wife had been *mugged*.

The ALP worker led the decoding discussion. The ABE tutor then wrote up the key words which had emerged. She focused on each word in turn, the context in which it had occurred, the shape and form of the word, and its associated meanings. Members then used the word to make a new statement. The challenge was the need to respond spontaneously and imaginatively to key words used by participants, and to ensure that any new words introduced related to the meaning of the discussion so far. The aim was to build on the communication between participants, and their eloquence in using the spoken word. Choosing key words and phrases and working on them in the group harnessed the energy generated by the discussion, deepened the analysis of themes, made participants aware of the power of their own words, and created a bridge from members' command of the spoken word to their problems in reading and writing. A follow-up programme focused on members' experience of schooling.

Other consultation and training

Throughout the life of the project, individuals, groups of field-workers, and students on training courses have telephoned or come to the ALP shop by arrangement, to consult ALP staff. This has been a significant part of their workload, and demand is quite heavy. A record was kept of the 25 consultations taking place between August and December, 1987, which shows that demand came from groups of university and college students, groups of adult and community education staff from other regions and countries, staff in community schools, ABE, health visiting, community and mental health work, new workers just taking up their posts, and new projects just getting off the ground.

Demand was for methods workshops on aspects of the ALP process, and particularly on making codifications and decoding, seminars on Freire's ideas, help with training the enquirer's own staff group, and practical advice on getting started.

The ALP response consisted either of organizing jointly planned workshops on the topic requested, or of having informal discussions with the enquirer.

This picture of a four-month period accurately reflects the quantity and range of demand for training and consultation based in the shop normally experienced by the project. Finally, the workers have responded to many requests to provide training events outwith Lothian Region, from Aberdeen in the north, to Peterborough in the south and Cork in the west.

One of the main attractions of ALP to local participants and fellow professionals has been its willingness to articulate the theory underlying its practice, and to make its methods available through training and consultation. In the course of these discussions, the ALP workers have relearned and further developed their ideas: the influence has been two-way.

CHAPTER 6

Reflections

The aim of this chapter is to reflect on the experience of ALP as a whole. An attempt is made to identify factors which have helped ALP to thrive, and implications for the management of innovation in adult learning, with a view to spreading the influence of such projects on the mainstream of education. This leads into a discussion of some significant themes in the work of ALP which have wider implications.

What has made ALP thrive?

ALP offers participants an approach to seeing and acting on the world. It encourages them to become curious, critical and creative. It begins with their existing ways of seeing, including felt needs, but doesn't simply cater to those needs. It helps people both to articulate and to change their values. It offers methods for constructing learning programmes and leading learning and action groups.

Within the framework of a clear set of educational ideas, ALP tries to integrate elements which are often split in our culture: theory and practice, structure and spontaneity, experience and knowledge, the local and the global.

Organizational reasons for ALP's success include: sponsorship by Lothian Region's Community Education Department, good leadership from the founding Community Education officer, good support from managers at fieldwork level, a programme of induction training for the workers appointed, the decision to deploy them as a team (a crucial factor), freedom to experiment, good choice of a base, and a sufficient supply of back-up resources.

Innovation and the mainstream

ALP began as a short-term specially funded project devoted to innovation in adult learning. Structurally it is outside the mainstream of education, and of community education. But operationally, ALP has forged collaborative links with workers in community education, health education, schools, adult basic education, further education, higher education, and voluntary organizations. The question here is: how should projects such as ALP relate to the mainstream?

The purpose of short-term funding is to create innovations which will have an impact on a broader field, making it more effective. The experience of ALP suggests that means need to be created to enable the innovation, from the outset, to influence the mainstream and receive feedback from it. One of the issues here is the relationship workers in mainstream settings are able to have with the innovation.

The ALP experience suggests three possible models for this relationship: infection, collaboration, and networking. Infection involves the new project in innovation, demonstration and fieldwork training. It can be achieved through training events, short-term placements, and consultation, with the new methods then being applied in mainstream settings. In the second model the innovative project enters into collaborative partnerships with other agencies. This is more of a peer relationship, in which the orientation and methods of each agency interact. The third model, networking, can begin to operate when the influence of the innovation has become widespread and resulted in workers in other settings having integrated and applied the innovation in their practice, and come to share its basic assumptions.

Location and management of innovative projects

How should a project like ALP be managed? Should it be located, as ALP is, in an area team, yet kept separate from the mainstream of generic work? Or should it be fully integrated from the outset into mainstream structures? Or should it – like the fieldwork teaching unit in community social work at Crossroads in Glasgow – be located in an independent voluntary organization, with a constitution, a membership, and an elected management committee, to which the workers are responsible? Or should it be run by a co-operative of workers directly accountable to the funding body?

ALP's present position in this respect may appear ambivalent: it is worker-led and local authority managed, with a voluntary co-ordinating body consisting of representatives of ALP groups and other members interested in the development of the project as a whole. Is a genuine partnership between funders, workers, and participants, such as ALP is attempting, possible?

Authority and responsibility

Amongst other things, ALP is about answering the questions: what is authority, how do we exercise it, and what is the difference between authority and authoritarianism? ALP struggles to restore the authority of the educator and of expert knowledge, while at the same time promoting the authority of the learner as co-educator. This leads ALP to make definite demands on members to participate actively in the learning process, to share responsibility for building the curriculum, and to lead learning and action groups.

Experience and knowledge

Taking responsibility and exercising one's own authority imply recognizing the authority of others. This is connected with the relationship between experience and knowledge. Since the 1960s there has been a swing of the pendulum away from high valuation of the knowledge possessed by experts towards valuing people's own experience. ALP struggles for a synthesis which values both. Experience on its own is not enough. The truth, as T. S. Eliot puts it in 'The Dry Salvages', is that all too often

We had the experience, but missed the meaning.

Four Quartets (Faber & Faber 1959)

In order to get at the meaning of our experiences, we need to reflect, to compare them with other (similar *and* different) experiences, and to do so we need to use existing concepts and insights, as well as helping to create new ones.

Theory and practice

Unlike social work and medicine, theory and practice in education tend to exist in separate worlds, with academic elaborations of theory posed against down-to-earth, anti-conceptual approaches to practice. ALP is committed to holding theory and practice in close productive tension. This has implications for training. Training bodies need to have ongoing engagement in fieldwork practice. Practice organizations need commitment to developing competence and standards. One way of integrating these two objectives would be to develop a constellation of field-work training units in practice settings.

Languages

Taking part in the ALP learning process places each participant at a set of interfaces between different languages. There is Paulo Freire's abstract theoretical language, the ALP workers' understanding of it and their attempts to translate it into English, and the language of each member of the group. There are issues of movement from concrete to abstract and from colloquial to formal, to say nothing of the different meanings individuals intend by the words and phrases they use. Far from being a problem in the negative sense, this can be a major source of learning. Ira Shor in discussion with Paulo Freire expresses one aspect of this matter clearly:

> My sense is that the teacher becomes more student-centred as he or she makes concrete the abstractions of academic language. The teacher learns how to existentialise philosophy, while the students learn how to philosophise experience.
>
> Freire and Shor 1987

Structure and spontaneity

There is an important tension in ALP between structure and spontaneity. Community Education practice, in reaction to traditional styles of schooling, further and higher education, has stressed informality, responsiveness and fluidity. ALP's approach is structured into a sequence of stages with clear tasks. Structure in ALP does not mean rigidity. The structure is held by the worker. At best it creates a sense of it being safe for participants to make spontaneous and authentic contributions to the theme being explored. The experienced worker is able, when appropriate, to let the structure go in the light of fruitful directions which may be opening up. But that does not mean that the process becomes aimless. Rigour should never be lost.

Some of these issues are illustrated in the following extract from a dialogue between Paulo Freire and Ira Shor:

PAULO: From the point of view of the students, a dialogical teacher who is incompetent and not serious provokes worse consequences than a serious and well-informed 'banking' educator.

IRA: What are the consequences?

PAULO: Ah! For example, the first one and the worst one is the testimony of irresponsibility, of intellectual irresponsibility.

IRA: That learning is impulsive and disorganized?

PAULO: Yes, that knowing is something that happens . . .

IRA: Out of the blue . . .

PAULO: And it is not! Knowing demands discipline! Knowing is something which demands many things from you, which makes you tired in spite of being happy. It is not something which just happens. Knowing, I repeat, is not a weekend on a tropical beach! . . .

IRA: You think that undirected 'liberating' classrooms present an image of aimless, flaky education which allows the authorities to claim that a strong central power is needed? Irresponsibility and disorder justify authoritarianism or help make it legitimate?

PAULO: It justifies their traditional methods . . .

Freire and Shor 1987

Oppression and alienation

In Freire's work in Brazil, Chile, and the former Portuguese colonies in Africa, the fundamental theme is oppression. In Gorgie Dalry, ALP workers have found that the most prevalent theme is alienation and the increasing privatization of people's lives. The growth of information technologies, for all the benefits they bring, gives a further twist to this theme. A major task implied by it is to encourage people to contact, communicate and collaborate with each other, and begin to see the possibility of taking risks and contributing to change in society.

Ethical, religious and political implications

The work of ALP, like that of Freire, has unmistakable ethical implications, declaring, for example, that people should be treated as subjects rather than objects of interest, manipulation or paternalism. There may also be religious implications, if religion is regarded as the search for values for living and ways of relating to each other and to the world. The following characteristics of ALP can be seen in this light: the attempt to involve as many people from the locality as possible: the identification and exploration of themes by participants; the carry-through from learning into action; the emphasis on taking responsibility and exercising authority; the stress on intentionality and shared purpose; the link with church house groups; the outward-turned orientation, seeking to relate to people from other cultures and areas, and those not yet involved; the emphasis on parenting and children; the provision of creches; and the regular social gatherings in the ALP shop, which are really celebrations of membership.

Ethical and religious considerations are linked with the political implications of Freire's thought. Much writing on Freire has stressed the political dimensions at the expense of the educational work. An attempt has been made here to redress the balance. It is hoped, however, that the political implications are clear. Freire's pedagogy is about facilitating people's emergence from their isolated position in the crowd, and their struggle to help create the good society, founded on dialogue and respect for each person as a subject, where people take responsibility for themselves and for others, where being is recognized as more important than having, where the need to have enough is seen as a necessary precondition for being to the full, and where the attempt by the few to accumulate great power and wealth is recognized as a denial of participation to the many.

Finally, Freire is realistic about the limited role of the educator in relation to these objectives. He emphasizes the need to avoid euphoric hope followed by cynical despair:

> Liberating education in general and the single classroom in particular cannot transform society by themselves. This limit needs to be repeated so that none of us mistake what dialogical learning means. Critical curiosity, some political awareness, democratic participation, habits of intellectual scrutiny, and interest in social change are realistic goals from inside a dialogic course.
>
> Freire and Shor 1987

Glossary

The following terms (in italics in text) are used by Paulo Freire or by ALP to describe aspects of the process and the thinking which informs it. Further discussions of them can be found in Chapter 2.

action outcome: Organized, sustained activity, arising from and involving members of an ALP *learning group*, to achieve a mutually agreed objective (e.g. Play in the Terraces, the Skills Exchange, etc.).

action reflection: Intentional human activity, involving thought on the part of
· participants about the implicit problems, circumstances, causes, interconnections and relationships, and their own awareness of these. Also called *praxis*. Splitting praxis into either of its constituent parts can lead to *activism* or *verbalism*. Action reflection is identified by Freire with work, love, and saying a true *word*.

activism: Action for action's sake, action without thought.

codification: Representation in pictorial, graphic, photographic, auditory, written, or dramatic form, or a combination of any or all of these, of a *significant situation* or situations in people's lives, in such a way as to include *contradictions* and embody *themes*. Can be used to refer to the process of encoding or to the object or sequence of objects produced.

co-educators: All participants in a *learning group* – members, co-ordinator, *observer*, *recorder*, *resource person* – are described by Freire as co-educators. They are both learners and teachers, educating each other. Dialogical learning is an attempt to resolve the teacher-student *contradiction*, but not by destroying the authority of the educator.

co-intentionality: A key feature of human *consciousness* is that it is intent upon the world, literally tending towards it in order to know it. Co-intentionality is Freire's term for the process by which people collaboratively focus their attention on a particular topic or aspect of reality. The means of co-intentionality is *dialogue*.

co-investigators: People in a locality who volunteer to work with the educators to investigate the life of the area, with a view to identifying *significant situations* and the *themes* implicit in them, organizing this thematic material, helping to prepare a sequence of *codifications* for *decoding*, and helping to create *learning programmes*.

conscientization: The process by which people are stimulated and encouraged to explore their reality and their awareness of it, so that their understanding of both reality and their own *consciousness* is deepened, and they begin to engage in *praxis*.

consciousness: For Freire, consciousness includes not only awareness, which can have a passive implication, but also an active sense of moving towards the world in order to know it. This involves the capacity for *investigation* and for understanding. It seems to include what we call conscience: the capacity to make value judgements about the world, others, and self. Finally, there is the capacity of consciousness to be aware of itself (consciousness of consciousness) which can lead to new perceptions. Freire conceives of a geology of stages or levels of consciousness, existing within each person, each of which represents a different orientation. He names these stages as MAGICAL, NAIVE (with possible backward deflection to FANATICAL or MYTHICAL consciousness), and CRITICAL. The particular characteristics of these stages are discussed in detail in Chapter 2.

contradictions: Contradictions are contrary, mutually opposing and sometimes antagonistic ideas or elements in people's lived reality which exist in tension with each other, and which are a source of potential energy for overcoming the *limit situations* or blocks in people's lives.

culture: Freire uses the term culture in its anthropological sense, not as we normally use it to refer to high culture (plays, poetry, opera) or popular culture (brass bands, trade union banners, popular celebrations). In this sense it denotes all aspects of the way of life of a human society or group: its language, art, technology, economy, means of exchange, family, kinship and class structures, ways of relating, religion and values. His use of the term culture is also infused with an awareness of its root meaning, which has to do with people acting on *nature* in order to produce the means of their continued existence. Culture is nature transformed by people's work. Freire regards it as important that oppressed people should be enabled to see that they are makers of culture.

culture circle/learning group: Freire uses the term culture circle, rather than class, to refer to a group of people engaged in *decoding* or taking part in a *dialogical learning programme*. Seating arrangements are likely to be circular or semicircular. He uses the word *culture* because he believes that people involved in this process are making culture. ALP uses the term learning group because culture circle is felt to be strange, as is the use of the word culture in its anthropological sense.

decoding: The process which occurs in a *culture circle* or *learning group* when its members are exploring a *codification*. It starts with description, then participants are encouraged to put themselves into the situation represented, and to recognize the situation in their own lives. It shades into analysis of both the codification and the life situation represented, involving movement to and from part to whole and from representation to reality. Throughout the process, *themes* emerge and begin to be identified.

dialogue: The communication that goes on between two or more people who are genuinely thinking and working together on some aspect of their lived reality. Dialogue is not a neutral descriptive word to describe verbal or other meaningful symbolic exchanges between people. It is a normative term denoting a desirable process of communication involving trust, collaboration, and active contribution (which can include silence). It also involves naming the world, or saying your own *word*, and is equated with true communication and with love.

intentionality: A key feature of human *consciousness* is that it is purposively intent upon the world. Freire's use of this word is infused with a sense of its root meaning, to tend towards. Consciousness tends or stretches towards the world. It can also be intent on itself (consciousness of consciousness).

intersubjectivity: The inter-experience, interaction, intercommunication, and interrelationships occurring between human beings through their *consciousness*. Freire's use of this term links it closely with *dialogue* and *co-intentionality*. He does not appear to include the specialized meanings found in psychoanalytic writings.

investigation: An unprejudiced exploration of some aspect of reality in its complexity, in order to understand it, including an understanding of its causes and connections. Freire uses such metaphors as to go into, to unveil, to understand, and to discover, to explain what he means by investigation, which should be carried out in *dialogue*, not in isolation.

key word (generative word): A key *word* in ALP usage is one which is charged with significance for people living in an area, or for members of a *learning group*. It is key in the sense that it unlocks or opens a way into the nature and meaning of some aspect of the world. When Freire's term generative word is used, two other meanings are added. First that the word generates discussion leading to other words or areas of concern. Secondly and more technically, it is a polysyllabic word which can be broken down into its constituent parts and used to create families of syllables from which participants can make up their own words. This technical possibility and the learning method based on it are described in Chapter 2. Some people argue that this possibility does not exist in English because it is not a syllabic language. In practice, ALP believes that it *is* possible to generate other words from an English key word, both by means of breaking it down and by association.

learning programme: The plans and materials for, and the actual experience of, finding out more about an agreed topic or *theme* in a *learning group*. The advance planning is done by the ALP workers, co-educators, and resource persons, and arises out of the processes of *investigation*, *codification*, and *decoding* described throughout the book.

limit situations: In the process of investigating their lived reality people come up against blocks which may be external, internal or a mixture of the two. At first they seem insurmountable, like walls. As the *investigation* deepens

and confidence grows, they begin to appear less overwhelming. Gradually participants come to recognize that these limits are places where new
possibilities begin, and that they can tackle the job of overcoming them.

nature: Freire links the term nature with the term *culture*. Nature is what is
there, or perhaps what would be there if people were not there: the sea, the
rivers, the land, the plants and animals, the sky – everything the world
consists of. Culture is nature transformed by people's work. This distinction is illuminating, but also problematic. First, human beings are themselves parts of nature, and secondly in many parts of the world the
transforming activity of human beings has gone so far that their products
seem to overwhelm nature. This does not destroy the value of the
distinction, but radically complicates our use of it. For Freire's image of
oppressed people experiencing themselves as submerged in *nature*, we
may have to substitute an image of submergence in alienating and
dehumanizing *culture*.

object: A thing or construct in the world capable of being perceived, known
or acted upon by people. Human beings can also be seen and treated as
objects and it is in this sense that Freire uses the term, which he contrasts
with the term *subject*. He formulates the contrast as follows: people can be
seen and treated either as subjects who know and act or as objects which
are known and acted upon. Freire normatively opts for the first and
opposes the second: this is the philosophical and ethical bedrock of his
approach to education, politics and living. He is opposed to all those
forces, whether of left, right, or centre, which treat people as objects of
beneficence or of manipulation.

Further, his use of the words *object* and *subject* is infused with the
meanings they have in the linguistic sequence subject, verb, object.
Subjects act on the world. Objects are acted upon. Though they can be
treated as objects by others, Freire believes that people can never be
reduced completely to the level of objects. But they can allow themselves
to become objects in certain respects, for example by becoming submerged in reality, by becoming caught up in fanatical movements, or by
confining their purposive activity to meeting their basic survival needs
only.

objectivism: Objectivism for Freire is a pitfall to be avoided. It consists of
believing that what is externally real is the only thing that is important,
and in downgrading human *consciousness*, which is our only means of
knowing the world. Freire believes that the objective world is real and
knowable. He describes its objective aspects as the empirical dimensions
of reality. Where he parts company with empiricism and objectivism is in
his emphasis on the fact that we know the world through our consciousness.

We must therefore maintain a double focus, on the objective aspects of
reality and on our subjective awareness. To know is to know our
consciousness, our selves, and the consciousness of our fellows, as well as
what is out there. Objectivism is an attempt to deny the simultaneity of
consciousness and the world. The opposite pitfall is *subjectivism*.

objectivity: The quality of the real world, its particular empirical nature or this-ness, which we can strive to know through our *subjectivity*.

observer: In a *culture circle* or *learning group*, one member who may be one of the team of educators or one of the *co-educators* has the task of observing the contributions and behaviour of individual participants, their interactions and the life of the group as a whole. Towards the end of the meeting the observer feeds back to the group his or her observations, and members have the opportunity to respond, accepting or rejecting the observations and using them to take the exploration further. The role of observer can be combined with that of *recorder*.

peak of action: A term used in ALP in relation to the task of preparing *codifications* of *significant situations*. A peak of action is a moment in the development of a significant situation in which the main actors are present, a maximum of significant action/interaction/communication is occurring, and in which some of the principal *contradictions* and *themes* are embodied. ALP photographers and artists hope to capture such moments.

praxis: The German word for practice, used by Marxists to denote political activity guided by a correct analysis of history and the present conjuncture. Freire has borrowed this term and given it his own meaning: praxis means action preceded, accompanied and followed by reflection, and/or reflection with an ongoing commitment to action. He uses praxis interchangeably with *action reflection*, and equates it with love, work, and naming the world.

problem-posing (problematizing): Freire sometimes calls his method of education the problem-posing method, by which he means that the *co-ordinator* often turns statements about the world made by members of a *culture circle* into questions to be explored. This implies an approach to education in which the educator's role is to encourage people to see reality not as taken-for-granted but as presenting itself in the form of problems or challenges to be worked at by the group. The co-ordinator is inviting participants to adopt a curious, investigative, questioning stance.

psycho-social: Freire uses the term psycho-social to characterize his educational method, which is based on the experience, feelings and thoughts of each participant; on their direct (past and present) relationships with others, in their lives and in the *learning group*; and on their relationship to the wider world as it impinges on their lives directly or indirectly.

recorder: In a *culture circle* or *learning group*, one participant (a member of the education team or one of the *co-educators*) may be given the task of recording the *themes* emerging during the discussion, sometimes noting down the actual words used by participants or the significant interactions occurring. This role is often combined with that of *observer*. The task of recorder is not the same as that of minute secretary at a committee meeting.

re-present: To re-present is to give back to a person or to members of a *learning group* something significant they have said, which is connected with the *theme* or aspect of reality being explored. It usually involves repeating some of the *key words* used, and is done at a moment when the educator feels it will be most helpful to the process of learning.

resource person: Resource person is the term used by ALP (Freire uses expert or specialist) to denote someone with specialist knowledge or skill in an area of interest to members of a *learning group*, for example a political theorist, a health visitor, a psychologist, a medical doctor, an economist, a poet, etc. The resource person is approached when a group has completed the process of *decoding* and created a sequence of *themes* about which they wish to know more. The resource person may be invited to participate in one or more sessions of a learning group, having first of all discussed it with ALP workers and/or *co-educators*, who will also explain the ALP method. The resource person is expected to present their expert knowledge in such a way as to dovetail with the group's present knowledge of and interest in the theme, within the sequence followed in each session of an ALP learning programme: say your own *word* (group members); presentation (resource person); dialogue (all).

significant situation: Conjunction of circumstances in the lives of people living in an area, in which events, interactions, and acts of communication are occurring. It involves elements of the physical circumstances (houses, streets, schools, work places, etc.) and the presence of people, in whatever roles and relationship and carrying out whatever tasks and responsibilities they have. It contains *contradictions*, and embodies *themes*. The choices of which situations are seen as significant are made in the process of *dialogue* between the educators and their local volunteer assistants, at the phase of initial *investigation*, and at later stages also by the participants in *decoding* discussions and *learning programmes*.

subject: The word subject is *not* used in its root sense of a person who is under domination (e.g. by a monarch or a state), but in a combination of its grammatical and philosophical senses. Philosophically a subject is a human being, the self, who thinks and knows. Grammatically the subject is that part of the sentence about which something is stated. Freire is particularly interested in the kind of sentence in which a named agent (subject) acts in some way (verb) on the world (object). Verbs, he point out, can be transitive (expressing an action which passes through into the object) or intransitive (expressing an action which does not pass through into the object). Freire takes these facts about the structure of human language as powerful metaphors expressing how human beings can relate to the world, and combines them with the philosophical meaning of subject already mentioned, to create his concepts of human beings as subjects who know and act on the world, transitivity (acting on the world), intransitivity (not acting on the world) and semi-intransitivity (acting on the world in relation only to basic survival needs).

subjectivism: The opposite pitfall to *objectivism*. At its extreme, subjectivism leads to the belief that only the self exists or is real (solipsism). Subjectivism is an imbalance in the relationship between human *consciousness* and the world, in which consciousness is given too much weight. It leads to misperception of the world and of others.

subjectivity: Human *consciousness*, through which we know the world, ourselves, and each other. In order to know the world truly we must also know our means of knowing it, our consciousness.

theme: By not giving excessive weight to objective reality, and by trying equally to avoid the distortions of *subjectivism*, Freire focuses our attention on the world as known by people through their *consciousness*, and through their purposive collaboration. That is, he focuses on the relationships between people and people, and people and the world. Such different orientations give rise to different languages. *Objectivism* strives to create a language neutrally and accurately describing what is there, purged (as if that were possible) of subjective interference. Subjectivism creates an imaginative language centring on the self as a lighthouse illuminating a dark or phantasmagoric outer space, purged of any steady sense of what exists out there. Freire's orientation leads him to create a language characterized by a constant to-ing and fro-ing between self and world, self and other, *subject* and *object*, part and whole, concrete and abstract. A key word of his language is theme. A theme is a human proposition about the world. It is an attempt to understand the world and our relationship to it, at some level of abstraction. Themes exist in the relationships between people and the world, at various levels of scale, temporally and spatially. Freire often refers to twin themes, and appears to hold that themes exist in relation to their opposites, for example domination and liberation, development and underdevelopment, etc. A generative theme is one the consideration of which by a *learning group* leads on to consideration of other themes which are implicit in it. Finally, themes are real, they exist, but they exist *for people*. They cannot be imposed on people. It is in this sense that basing an approach to education on people's themes diverges sharply from the pedagogic tradition of determining the shape and content of an education programme purely in terms of the logic of a specialism. Themes emerge and are named in the dialogue which goes on between people who are co-intent on some aspect of reality.

verbalism: Mere talk; reflection without action; a purely intellectual interest in a topic without engagement or commitment to what it means to people, or to its action implications for the speaker.

word: The name of the product of the core human act of naming the world. This is seen as the distinguishing essence of our humanity, which makes us different from animals. It is associated with God's creation and naming of the world as described in the book of Genesis. That is, naming and creating are intimately associated. Words are our key means of knowing the world and of acting on it in order to transform it. That is, naming and acting on the world reflectively are intimately associated. Words are not to be dichotomized from the human being who is using them to name the world. A word can, therefore, be true or false, that is it represents an attempt to reveal the world or to obscure it, and to reveal or obscure the true intentions of the speaker. Saying a true word, for Freire, is a characteristic of *praxis*, love, and work.

Select bibliography

Brown, Cynthia (1975) *Literacy in 30 Hours: Paulo Freire's Process in North-East Brazil*. London, Writers and Readers Publishing Cooperative.

Collins, Denis (1977) *Paulo Freire: His Life, Works and Thought*. New York, Paulist Press.

Costigan, Margaret (1980) *You Have the Third World Inside You: an interview with Paulo Freire*. Edinburgh, Workers' Educational Association.

Freire, Paulo (1972) *Cultural Action for Freedom*. Harmondsworth, Penguin.

Freire, Paulo (1972) *Pedagogy of the Oppressed*. Harmondsworth, Penguin.

Freire, Paulo (1974) *Education for Critical Consciousness*. London, Sheed and Ward. (Also published as *Education: the Practice of Freedom*. London, Writers and Readers Publishing Cooperative, 1976.)

Freire, Paulo (1978) *Pedagogy in Process: the Letters to Guinea-Bissau*. New York, Seabury Press.

Freire, Paulo (1985) *The Politics of Education: Culture, Power and Liberation*. London, Macmillan.

Freire, Paulo, and Macedo, Donaldo (1987) *Literacy: Reading the Word and the World*. London, Routledge and Kegan Paul.

Freire, Paulo, and Shor, Ira (1987) *A Pedagogy for Liberation: dialogues on transforming education*. London, Macmillan.

Hope, Anne, and Timmel, Sally (1985) *Training for Transformation: A Handbook for Community Workers, Books 1, 2 & 3*. Gweru, Zimbabwe, Mambo Press.

Kirkwood, Colin, and Griffiths, Sally (1984) *Adult education and the Unemployed*. Edinburgh, Workers' Educational Association.

Mackie, Robert (1980) *Literacy and Revolution: the Pedagogy of Paulo Freire*. London, Pluto Press.

Shor, Ira (1987) *Critical Teaching and Everyday Life*. Chicago, University of Chicago Press.

Shor, Ira (1987) *Freire for the Classroom: A Sourcebook for Liberatory Teaching*. Portsmouth, USA, Boynton Cook.

Digest of statistics

Total number of courses,
    investigations and groups   31
Total of enrolments   1,579
Total of participants in
    training and consultation   2,100

Breakdown of enrolments

	No.	% of total
Total males	692	43.8
Total females	887	56.2
Total married	797	50.5
Total single	709	44.9
Total widowed	73	4.6
Teenagers	11	0.7
20/30s	1091	69.2
40/50s	347	21.9
60s and over	130	8.2
Paid employment	592	37.5
Unemployed	498	31.5
Students	64	4.0
Housewives	331	21.0
Retired	94	6.0
Local	1080	68.4
Outsiders	499	31.6

The period covered is September 1979–November 1987.

GROUP/YEAR

	Living in Gorgie Dalry Investigation 1979–80	Family Today You & the School On being Scottish 1981	Unemployed Group 1981	Pubs 1981–82	Tynecastle School Parents 1981–82	Writers Workshop 1981–87	Welfare Rights Group 1982	Manifesto Group 1982
Gender:								
Male	11	17	6	22	22	70	6	2
Female	31	45	2	8	22	52	5	6
Marital status:								
Married	29	46	5	22	44	40	2	2
Single	12	14	3	6	–	82	8	5
Widowed	1	2	–	2	–	–	1	1
Age:								
Teens	–	–	–	–	–	2	8	–
20/30s	38	54	7	14	30	94	3	7
40/50s	2	5	1	12	14	24	–	–
60s & over	2	3	–	4	–	2	–	1
Occupational status:								
Paid employment	15	11	–	21	26	53	11	5
Unemployed	4	9	8	3	10	49	–	2
Student	2	1	–	2	–	15	–	–
Housewife	19	38	–	1	8	3	–	–
Retired	2	3	–	3	–	2	–	1
Residence:								
Local	39	55	6	23	44	68	11	8
Outsider	3	7	2	7	–	54	–	–
Total enrolments:	42	62	8	30	44	122	11	8

GROUP/YEAR

		Play in the Terraces 1982–83	Skills Exchange 1982–87	Photo Workshop 1982–87	Health & Well-being Investigation 1982–83	New Technology Investigation 1982–83	Computer Workshop 1983	Programme for Unemployment & Loose End Centre 1983–84	Living Memory Project 1983–87
Gender:	Male	5	78	100	10	6	6	39	10
	Female	29	150	54	25	1	3	21	7
Marital status:	Married	28	94	43	24	3	3	7	14
	Single	2	128	110	8	4	5	53	2
	Widowed	4	6	1	3	–	1	–	14
Age:	Teens	–	–	–	–	–	–	–	–
	20/30s	27	182	129	27	7	5	52	–
	40/50s	3	38	18	5	–	2	8	–
	60s & over	4	8	7	3	–	2	–	30
Occupational status:	Paid employment	5	72	94	7	3	–	–	–
	Unemployed	2	90	88	9	4	7	60	–
	Student	–	10	14	–	–	–	–	–
	Housewife	23	48	5	16	–	–	–	–
	Retired	4	8	3	3	–	2	–	–
Residence:	Local	34	150	66	28	4	5	39	20
	Outsider	–	78	88	7	3	4	21	10
Total enrolments:		34	228	154	35	7	9	60	30

GROUP/YEAR

		Women & Well-being 1983–85	Church House Groups 1982–87	Unemployment Investigation 1984	Workshops for Unemployed 1985	Photo Archive 1985–86	Parents & Authority 1985	Music Workshop 1986	Skills Exchange Short Courses 1986–87
Gender:	Male	–	124	11	52	7	2	2	12
	Female	44	176	4	28	5	24	7	45
Marital status:	Married	30	204	2	12	1	26	5	24
	Single	13	63	13	68	11	–	4	30
	Widowed	1	33	–	–	–	–	–	3
Age:	Teens	1	–	–	–	–	–	–	–
	20/30s	40	83	13	62	12	26	9	39
	40/50s	3	165	2	12	–	–	–	17
	60s & over	–	52	–	6	–	–	–	1
Occupational status:	Paid employment	15	172	–	–	1	–	7	33
	Unemployed	6	26	15	80	10	3	–	8
	Student	–	12	–	–	1	–	–	1
	Housewife	23	64	–	–	–	23	2	13
	Retired	–	26	–	–	–	–	–	2
Residence:	Local	31	217	8	58	8	25	9	40
	Outsider	13	83	7	22	4	1	–	17
Total enrolments:		44	300	15	80	12	26	9	57

	Parents Centre 1986–87	TV Programmes (Training) 1986–87	Popular TV Soaps & Ads Humour on the box 1986–87	Living with Teenagers 1987	Fresh Start 1987	ALP/ABE 1987	Photography for Unemployed 1987
Gender: Male	5	9	21	2	5	5	18
Female	35	9	17	6	2	4	14
Marital status: Married	39	11	16	8	2	3	8
Single	1	7	22	–	5	6	24
Widowed	–	–	–	–	–	–	–
Age: Teens	–	–	–	–	–	–	–
20/30s	40	14	25	8	7	7	30
40/50s	–	4	9	–	–	2	1
60s & over	–	–	4	–	–	–	1
Occupational status: Paid employment	4	7	20	3	–	4	–
Unemployed	2	7	6	1	7	4	31
Student	–	–	6	–	–	–	–
Housewife	34	4	2	4	–	1	–
Retired	–	–	4	–	–	–	1
Residence: Local	39	14	12	4	4	1	10
Outsider	1	4	26	4	3	8	22
Total enrolments:	40	18	38	8	7	9	32

Index

access, 30, 31
action outcome, 2, 6, 7, 11, 14, 17, 18, 19, 21, 24, 31, 67, 68, 70, 99, 101, 117, 118, 126, 133, 135, 139
action reflection, 12, 14, 21, 37, 38, 43, 68, 123, 125, 138, 139, 143
activism, 40, 139
Adult Basic Education, 24, 130, 131, 134
Adult Learning Project (ALP), 1, 15, 25, 26, 28, 30, 31, 119, 120, 124, 125, 126, 127, 129, 131, 133, 134, 137, 138, 139, 141
Alexander Report, 29
alienation, 137
ALP Coordinating Group, 20, 22, 25, 32, 114, 116, 135
ALP process, 6, 7, 18, 23, 24, 48, 125, 128, 136
ALP shop, 17
authority, 23, 30, 46, 54, 64, 65, 66, 79, 80, 81, 82, 83, 89, 91, 93, 94, 96, 97, 114, 123, 135, 137, 138, 139

banking education, 39
barriers, 54, 64, 89
Black Papers, 28
Brazil, 24, 26, 32, 33, 34, 40, 46

Britain, 26, 29, 95, 96, 105
Buber, Martin, 34

Careers Service, 24
case studies, 6, 15, 47, 48, 49, 101
Catholicism, 32, 34
Chile, 26, 33, 128, 137
Church house groups, 18, 126, 138
class, 38
codification, 6, 7, 9, 10, 11, 12, 14, 17, 18, 42, 44, 51, 52, 56, 59, 62, 64, 70, 71, 80, 84, 115, 116, 125, 130, 131, 139, 140, 141, 143
co-educators, 123, 128, 135, 139, 141, 143, 144
co-intentionality, 39, 127, 139, 141, 145
co-investigators, 6, 7, 8, 9, 10, 11, 12, 14, 15, 40, 45, 49, 50, 51, 68, 69, 70, 79, 80, 81, 82, 83, 84, 89, 139
communication, 38, 68, 69, 73, 76, 77, 99, 106, 131, 137, 141
community, 30, 32, 101, 102
community action, 27
community control, 30, 32
community education, 1, 15, 20, 21, 22, 26, 29, 31, 109, 128, 129, 130, 131, 133, 134, 136
community schools, 28

comprehensivization, 28
conscience, 36, 140
conscientization, 43, 45, 46, 140
consciousness, 36, 37, 38, 39, 40,
    43, 139, 140, 141, 142, 144, 145
Conservative Party, 27
contract, 73, 78, 129
contradictions, 10, 11, 12, 20, 31,
    40, 42, 45, 51, 72, 83, 99,
    110, 111, 127, 139, 140, 143,
    144
co-ordinator, 11, 12, 42, 43, 47,
    48, 62, 63, 64, 70, 78, 86,
    114, 129, 139, 143
culture, 33, 35, 36, 45, 89, 90, 91,
    92, 93, 94, 95, 96, 97, 98, 99,
    105, 133, 138, 140, 142
culture circle, 33, 42, 43, 44, 140,
    143
curriculum building, 6, 7, 12, 64,
    80, 89, 128, 135

de Chardin, Teilhard, 34
decoding, 6, 7, 10, 11, 12, 17, 18,
    19, 24, 42, 44, 45, 47, 51, 52,
    62, 63, 64, 68, 70, 78, 79, 80,
    85, 86, 89, 113, 115, 116,
    124, 128, 130, 131, 140, 141,
    144
dependence and independence,
    101, 106
dialectic, 39, 46
dialogue, 10, 11, 12, 13, 18, 31,
    33, 38, 39, 40, 42, 45, 48, 64,
    65, 73, 75, 96, 97, 105, 117,
    121, 125, 126, 127, 129, 137,
    138, 139, 141, 144, 145
disadvantage, 30, 31

Edinburgh, 2, 95, 98
Edinburgh District Council, 4,
    115, 116
education, 26, 28, 31, 35, 39, 40,
    66, 124, 127, 133, 134, 138,
    142, 143, 145
Eliot, T. S., 135
empiricism, 39, 142

experience and knowledge, 65, 80,
    92, 96, 99, 127, 133, 135, 144

Family Today, 17, 47, 48, 65
Fanon, Frantz, 35
Freire, Paulo, 2, 6, 13, 15, 18, 21,
    24, 25, 26, 32, 33, 34, 35, 36,
    37, 38, 39, 40, 42, 43, 44, 45,
    127, 128, 131, 136, 137, 138,
    139, 140, 142, 143, 144
Fresh Start, 23, 24
Fromm, Erich, 35

generic community education, 20,
    30, 134
Geneva, 34
Gorgie City Farm, 4
Gorgie Dalry, 1, 2, 4, 6, 17, 21,
    26, 32, 52, 70, 99, 106, 109,
    114, 115, 137
Gorgie Dalry Housing
    Association, 4
Guevara, Che, 35
Guinea-Bissau, 34

Hassan, Janet, 92, 93, 94, 96, 97,
    100
Health and Unemployment, 20,
    47, 68, 70, 78
Health and Well-being, 19, 47, 68,
    78
Health Visitors, 24
Hearts Football Club, 2
Hegel, Georg, 35
Husserl, Edmund, 35

illiteracy, 33
individualism, 27
intentionality, 37, 141
intersubjectivity, 39, 141
intransitivity, 36, 37, 144
investigation, 2, 7, 8, 14, 15, 17,
    18, 19, 21, 31, 38, 39, 44, 45,
    47, 48, 49, 68, 79, 99, 103,
    117, 128, 140, 141, 144
isolation, 52, 57, 77, 110
issue-based education, 2, 30

Kenya, 94, 95, 96
key word (generative word), 12, 24, 40, 44, 130, 131, 141, 144

language, 38, 39, 40, 99, 130, 136, 144, 145
learning group, 17, 49, 120, 128, 129, 133, 135, 139, 140, 141, 143, 144, 145
learning programme, 2, 6, 7, 11, 13, 14, 17, 18, 21, 24, 31, 47, 48, 64, 65, 67, 68, 70, 72, 79, 80, 90, 92, 99, 101, 110, 113, 115, 116, 117, 122, 126, 128, 133, 140, 141, 144
liberation theology, 32, 34, 38
limit situations, 45, 46, 140, 141
literacy, 33, 40, 42, 43, 130
Living in Gorgie Dalry, 15, 19, 47, 48, 101
Living in Wester Hailes, 24
Living Memory Project, 20, 68, 70, 115
Living with a Toddler, 24
Living with Change in Gorgie Dalry, 24, 116
Loose-end Activity Centre, 20, 68, 71, 78
Lothian Regional Council, 1, 18, 21, 22, 24, 109, 115, 130, 133
love 35, 139, 141, 143, 145
Lukacs, Georg, 35

Manifesto Group, 17
Manpower Services Commission, 28
Mao Tse-Tung, 35
Marx, Karl, 35
Marxism, 27, 28, 38, 143
massification, 37, 38
Memmi, Albert, 35
moments of life, 8, 50, 69
Mounier, Emmanuel, 32, 34
mutuality, 101, 106, 109, 110, 128, 132

nature, 35, 36, 140, 142, 143
networking, 51, 130, 134

new technology, 19
Nyerere, Julius, 35

object, 35, 36, 37, 40, 138, 142, 144, 145
objectivism, 39, 142, 144, 145
objectivity, 39, 143
observer, 8, 9, 12, 44, 64, 70, 129, 139, 143
On Being Scottish, 17, 47, 48, 65
open questions, 8, 11, 42, 50, 62, 63, 126
outreach, 30, 31

parenting in different cultures, 23, 47, 90
Parents and Authority, 23, 47, 79
Parents Centre, 23, 99, 101, 110, 111
paternalism, 26, 27
peak of action, 10, 143
Photo Workshop, 18, 22, 70, 101, 105, 114, 115, 116, 117, 118, 123
photography, 10, 17, 22, 42, 44, 51, 52, 56, 60, 71, 85, 105, 114, 115, 116, 120, 121, 123, 143
Play in the Terraces, 17, 101, 103, 104, 122, 123, 139
Pope John XXIII, 34
popular television, 23
post-literacy, 44
power and powerlessness, 64
Practitioners Skills Exchange, 22, 128, 129
praxis, 38, 139, 140, 143, 145
primary source investigation, 6, 7, 15
problem-posing (problematizing), 39, 42, 143
psycho-social, 143

Recife, 33
recorder, 8, 48, 64, 70, 86, 139, 143
rehabilitation, 4
relevance, 30, 31

re-present, 9, 42, 121, 124, 143

resource person (expert), 14, 45, 48, 64, 65, 67, 68, 73, 75, 78, 79, 80, 91, 94, 97, 98, 139, 141, 144

responsibility, 14, 38, 117, 122, 135, 137, 138

risk and security, 79, 84, 85, 86, 90

Sartre, Jean-Paul, 35

Scotland, 20, 27, 29, 60, 114, 128

Scottish identity, 60, 67

Scottish Office, 1

Scottish self-government, 27

secondary source investigation, 6, 7, 15, 40

Shandon, 4

Shor, Ira, 136, 137, 138

Sieley, Sarah, 94, 95, 96, 100

significant situation, 9, 42, 139, 143, 144

Skills Exchange, 17, 22, 101, 106, 107, 108, 123, 128, 139

St Bride's Community Centre, 20, 23, 70, 111, 112

structure and spontaneity, 25, 114, 127, 133, 136

subject, 35, 40, 138, 142, 144, 145

subjectivism, 39, 142, 144, 145

subjectivity, 39, 143, 145

Tanzania, 34

tenement, 4, 52, 116

Thatcher, Margaret, 27, 28

theme, 9, 10, 11, 12, 14, 17, 21, 31, 32, 36, 38, 39, 40, 42, 43, 44, 45, 48, 50, 51, 52, 59, 63, 64, 67, 68, 72, 75, 80, 83, 84, 89, 101, 112, 113, 115, 116, 120, 127, 133, 136, 137, 138, 139, 141, 143, 144, 145

theory and practice, 133, 135, 136

Tillich, Paul, 34

trade unionism, 27

training and consultation, 20, 21, 22, 25, 125, 126, 127, 128, 129, 130, 131, 132, 134, 136

transitivity, 36, 38, 144

Urban Aid, 1, 18, 31, 32

USA, 33

verbalism, 38, 139, 145

welfare state, 26

welfarism, 26, 27

Well-Woman Centre, 20

Wester Hailes, 2

Women and Well-being, 20, 23, 47, 68, 72, 73, 76, 77, 79, 120, 123

women's liberation, 27

word, 13, 38, 43, 65, 112, 121, 130, 131, 139, 141, 144, 145

Workers Educational Association (WEA), 2

World Council of Churches, 34

Writers Workshop, 18, 22, 101, 112, 113, 114, 116, 117, 118

You and the School, 17, 47, 48, 65, 66